Breaking Up the Bank:
Rethinking an Industry Under Siege

Breaking Up
the Bank:
Rethinking an Industry
Under Siege

Lowell L. Bryan

DOW JONES-IRWIN
Homewood, Illinois 60430

Acquisitions editor: Jim Childs
Project editor: Jane Lightell
Production manager: Stephen K. Emry
Jacket photograph: Patti McConville/Image Bank
Compositor: Publication Services
Typeface: 11/13 Century Schoolbook
Printer: Arcata Graphics/Kingsport

LIBRARY OF CONGRESS
Library of Congress Cataloging-in-Publication Data

Bryan, Lowell L.
    Breaking up the bank: rethinking an industry under seige/Lowell L. Bryan
      p. cm.
    Includes index.
    ISBN 1-556-23144-X:
    1. Banks and banking—United States—State supervision. 2. Banks and banking—United States—Government guaranty of deposits.
3. Bank mergers—United States. I. Title.
HG2491.B78 1988
332.1'0973—dc19   88-14908
                                                CIP

Printed in the United States of America
1 2 3 4 5 6 7 8 0 K 5 4 3 2 1 0 9 8

This book is dedicated to the memory of my father
Lyman Lowell Bryan

INTRODUCTION

Just a few years ago the banking industry in the United States was a comfortable business. Customers were undemanding. Profits were high. Credit losses were barely noticeable.

Today, banks are under siege. The industry's underlying economics are weak and deteriorating. Credit losses are enormous and growing. As if that were not enough, a new technology for lending—*structured securitized credit*—threatens the industry's very franchise. What happened?

Essentially, we introduced intense competition into the banking industry without fundamentally rethinking either how banks should be regulated or how they should be managed. We forgot that the stability and profitability of the banking system in the environment after the Great Depression of the 1930s was founded on regulation that prevented competition and essentially forced customers to use banks, like it or not. We forgot that regulation protected banks at the expense of some of their customers. Two customer groups, in fact, subsidized the system: large depositors (primarily individuals) were not paid the full value for their deposits because of interest rate restrictions, and high-quality borrowers (primarily corporations) paid more for their loans than their risk would justify.

These subsidies were hard to spot because of the cost structure of the banks. Just as in a utility or a university, most of the costs of running the entire bank were shared and used for the benefit of all customers. Nobody tried to ensure that specific customers (paying specific prices for the services they received) were benefited by specific expenditures, because regulation made that unnecessary. This "bundled" banking system, founded on customer cross-subsidies, worked because relatively undifferentiated service levels from bank to bank gave customers little choice between banks and because oligopolistic pricing practices provided the revenues to support the system. Bank profitability was high and relatively uniform, and the banking system was sound. It was a comfortable life for banks.

But then the "protected" system began to be undermined. In the United States the large depositors and high-quality borrowers who were subsidizing the banking system began to explore alternatives offered to them by securities firms. For many, "securitization" offered better value. Large depositors moved in droves to money market mutual funds, while high-quality borrowers moved to commercial paper. This migration began in the early 1970s, accelerated in the late 1970s, and grew explosively in the 1980s. The regulatory structure was loosened a bit to make banks more competitive—and, in fact, banks have been able to regain position in some areas (e.g., money market accounts have slowed the outflow of money to money market funds). But to do so they have had to forfeit their customer subsidies. As a result, the banks have lost much of their ability to cross-subsidize some customer groups with revenues earned from others.

Now that competition has been introduced into the system, and cross-customer subsidies are becoming a thing of the past, we need to design a new banking system that is founded not on protective regulation and cross-subsidies, but on providing fair value to each customer. Yet both regulators and bankers cling to practices that are based upon the old post-Depression model. Unfortunately, that model is becoming less and less practical.

Consider, for example, that one of the model's principal foundations is federal deposit insurance. In the wake of the stock market crash of October 1987, commentators cited the deposit insurance system as one of the main reasons why that crash was unlikely to lead to a repeat of the Great Depression. But the terrible truth is that the combination of federal deposit insurance and competition leads to unsound credit practices that could indeed bring down much of our financial system. A large minority of banks and thrifts are using federal deposit insurance and high deposit interest rates to attract deposits, which they lack the credit skills to deploy as safely as loans. Without cross-customer subsidies, these weak players are becoming more and more reliant on what is, in effect, a government insurance subsidy.

While there is little doubt that our existing system would collapse without federal deposit insurance, there is also little doubt that the system will soon collapse under its burden of bad loans. The Federal Savings and Loan Insurance Corporation fund (FSLIC) is already bankrupt; the costs of cleaning up the mess in just the thrift industry could easily approach $100 billion if we were to face up to it today. If the United States were to have a severe recession, it is quite possible that even the Federal Deposit Insurance Company (FDIC) fund , the guarantor of the commercial banking system's deposits, could be severely strained.

Indeed, it seems increasingly likely that when the nation does face up to the costs of combining competition with deposit insurance, the cost to taxpayers will be almost unbelievably high. These high costs could lead to damaging reregulation, which could both suddenly decrease the credit available to the public and complete the destruction of the industry. If competent institutions are swept up in a "witch hunt" of stifling reregulation, our whole financial economy could be severely damaged, and well-managed banks and thrifts, who add enormous value to their customers and the nation, could be unfairly penalized. Frankly, rather than reregulation, we need a new regulatory framework—a framework designed for a competitive environment.

But it is not just obsolete regulation that is to blame. Many bankers, too, are at fault for clinging to old methods of management. For example, many continue to operate as if they still had oligopolistic control of their pricing. They spend money and run their banks as if they were still sheltered from the marketplace and still had some customers willing to subsidize others. But those days are gone forever, and the old management approaches are positively suicidal in this new competitive environment.

Thus, we need to rethink both banking and its regulatory structure. We need a new model.

Fortunately, a new technology for lending has been created that can help make the transition to a fundamentally different, and better, financial system. This new technology for lending is called *structured securitized credit*, and it is better on all counts than the traditional lending system. It is growing very rapidly precisely because it is a superior technology—one that, in fact, is rendering the traditional banking system obsolete. It has essentially been developed by nonbankers and, left on its own, will help accelerate the forces outlined earlier that are destroying the classic banking industry. On the other hand, managed differently, it could breathe new life into the industry's existing franchise.

Whereas the old model depended on the cross-subsidy of deposits and loans, the structured securitized credit process would enable the industry to separate the depositing and lending functions and to build unbundled businesses around the specific activities in which each bank can add the most value, at the lowest price, to customers. Once each bank is broken into its component parts, those parts can be reassembled into a financial institution that can succeed in today's free-for-all competitive environment. At the same time, structured securitized credit also provides the potential for protecting depositors through regulation without subsidizing unsound lending practices. It thus offers the potential for both a new management model and a new regulatory model—both designed for competition.

This book has three parts. The first part looks at the theory behind the traditional banking model and explains why that model no longer works. The second part presents a new model—built on structured securitized credit—for managing and regulating banks. The final part describes the roles this model would offer to banks of different sizes and the actions individual institutions should take today to prepare for the new roles.

I have written with the United States commercial banking system uppermost in my mind. However, the forces described here are also at work in Europe and Japan, albeit more slowly. My best estimate is that European banking today is at roughly the stage of evolution that U.S. banking was in the late 1970s. Thus, much of the thinking in the book is likely to be equally relevant to these banks, particularly as they move closer and closer to 1992 (the date set for allowing more equal competition by European banks outside their home countries). Indeed, the book might even help European banks avoid a few pitfalls.

In Japan, whose regulatory structure is more like the U.S. system, there are many parallels but also many differences. The most important difference is that unsound credit practices in Japan have led not to credit losses, but rather to what is essentially government-supported financial speculation in stocks and real estate. Thus, the problem in Japan is different; but the solution, based on structured securitized credit, could be similar.

ACKNOWLEDGMENTS

While the opinions expressed in this book are my own, I want to acknowledge the broad support I received from McKinsey & Company and others.

In particular, I would like to thank three fellow McKinsey directors: Mike Bulkin (head of the New York Office), Don Waite (head of McKinsey's worldwide financial institutions practice), and Ron Daniel (managing director of our Firm). The three of them, along with my wife, Debbie, provided me with both the encouragement and the support I needed to undertake this effort.

Much of the book is drawn from the results of a self-funded project launched by McKinsey & Company under my direction in late 1986. It was aimed at gaining a better understanding of the problems in the U.S. credit system, the impact of securitized credit on that system, and how the credit system in the United States is likely to evolve. The primary purpose of the project was to improve McKinsey's ability to serve its extensive client base of financial institutions, including money center banks, securities firms, and insurance companies. A second purpose was to contribute constructively to the public dialogue on what changes in laws and regulations are required to ensure an efficient, effective, and safe financial system. During this project, we interviewed literally hundreds of individuals, including bankers, investment bankers, lawyers, and accountants, in addition to members of McKinsey. We also held discussions with regulators and the staff of the Senate Banking Committee. Juan Ocampo is another McKinsey partner who took a leadership role in the project. Additional members of the project team included Guy Moszkowski, Jim Rosenthal, Kewsong Lee, and Sameer Shah. In particular, Juan and Jim spent considerable time with me discussing the full, long-term implications of credit securitization.

We received substantial help from two New York lawyers—

Neil Baron of Booth & Baron and Morris Simpkin of Siller, Wilk, Mencher, & Simpkin—on legal issues related to securitizing credit.

In helping with the actual preparation of the book, I would like to thank a number of McKinsey professionals. In particular, I would like to thank Jack Stephenson, who oversaw the analysis of the numbers, contributed to the thinking about what the numbers meant, and led the drafting of the exhibits. Bernard Gunther and Arthur Chin of McKinsey's Cambridge Systems Center used their systems skills to compile the massive analysis of FDIC data appearing throughout the book. The Stamford Office of McKinsey, led by Dolf DiBiasio, provided me with a "home" to draft the manuscript. Helen Stern-Richter also helped in undertaking literary searches and gathering facts. Beth Manzi oversaw the production of the charts of exhibits.

In the first several chapters of the book I drew upon some research undertaken by Tom Steiner of McKinsey (New York) on the profitability trends of commercial banks in the early 1980s. I also drew upon some work by George Feiger of McKinsey (San Francisco) on economies of scale in banking.

Brook Manville, of McKinsey; Patricia Haskell, my literary agent; and Jim Childs, the editor of the book, were all very helpful in thinking through the content and broad messages of the book. Dominic Casserley and Jim Rosenthal were particularly helpful in viewing the manuscript of the book, and many of their comments have resulted in changes in the text. Christine Butler typed the first draft and the redrafts—exhibiting singular patience, and, often, the ability to intuit which of the two or three alternate sentences that I had written was the one I had really meant. She made me look better on film, too (see the cover photo).

I would also like to thank my administrative assistant, Susan Pistilli, for help in keeping the entire effort coordinated and for her charm and wit, which helped to sustain my energy while writing the book under a very tight deadline.

Finally, I would like to thank Susan Benthall, a free-lance writer who worked closely with me in the actual writing and rewriting of the book. Susan has an extraordinary ability to improve not only my writing but my thinking as well.

CONTENTS

PART 1

AN INDUSTRY UNDER SIEGE

CHAPTER 1

THE ECONOMIC THEORY
OF A BANK

Modern banking began in medieval Europe, when money changers and goldsmiths decided to use the money given to them for safekeeping to earn additional profits for themselves. Operating purely as depository institutions, these early bankers always had plenty of cash available for any depositor who wanted his cash back, while most of the money they held for safekeeping simply stayed in their safes. In fact, they soon discovered they could lend the idle money out and earn interest, provided they kept enough cash to pay off any depositor who demanded his money back. Banks around the world still employ this same fundamental business system.

Of course, this system breaks down if every depositor wants his money at the same time. But this should not happen if the pool of depositors is large enough, since not all of them should need cash at the same time. On the other hand, if depositors as a group lose confidence in their banks for any reason, they naturally want their money simultaneously, and a bank panic ensues.

Throughout the history of capitalism, up to the 1930s, bank panics were common in the United States and Europe; in fact, they recurred with disturbing regularity. Then, following the Great Depression, national governments around the world found various means of preventing bank panics. For the most part this meant regulating credit extension practices, establishing capital adequacy guidelines, limiting competition, and providing direct or implicit government guarantees to depositors. The regulatory framework adopted during the Depression by the United States included all of these elements. For example, bank regulators were granted direct oversight over lending practices, the quality of the loan portfolio, and the amount of capital that a bank or bank holding company was required to maintain.

To further stabilize the system the government granted special regulatory and legal charters that restricted competition and thereby forced customers to use banks. Deposit regulations were of particular importance. Commercial banks were granted a checking power monopoly and were prohibited from paying interest on demand deposits. They were also limited in the interest they could pay on savings accounts. Thrifts had an interest ceiling, too, but they were permitted to pay one-quarter of a percent more and as a result had a high share of savings deposits. To further limit competition regulators imposed geographic barriers to doing business (e.g., branching restrictions, prohibitions on interstate banking). These essentially caused the industry to operate as a series of local oligopolies and caused banks' underlying characters to be shaped by their geographic scope (e.g., money center, regional, community). Finally, the Glass-Steagall Act forced the separation of securities and banking industries. Commercial banks had to divest most of their securities activities and refrain from participating in most securities businesses.

The final guarantor of stability and profitability was the combination of federal deposit insurance and the lender-of-last-resort function of the Federal Reserve. This enabled the industry to operate safely with higher leverage than other intermediaries (e.g., finance companies).

The boundaries between banking and nonbanking activities were defined further by two later legislative changes. The Bank Holding Company Act of 1956 regulated multibank holding companies and limited the growth of interstate banking through holding companies. The Bank Holding Company Act of 1970 placed bank holding companies under Federal Reserve regulation giving it, among other powers, the authority to define which activities banks were permitted to engage in. In combination these holding company acts also served to prevent bank holding companies from owning commercial concerns and vice versa.

This combination of regulations created a sound banking system, albeit an artificially sound one. We have avoided bank panics for five decades. We have also in that time built a bank economic model with some very distinctive characteristics that reflect the regulatory framework. This model is based upon bundling together customer revenues, bank expenses, and shareholder capital into a single, integrated, economic enterprise. Most bankers today do not question whether or not this "bundled" economic model makes sense; most of them know of no other.

The model has three fundamental, implicit assumptions (Exhibit 1-1): (1) Each bank will have a stable pool of revenue, known as the net interest margin, sufficient to cover all reasonable costs and to provide reasonable returns on capital; (2) Given that net interest margin, each bank can devote most of its operating cost base to expenditures related to the common service of all its customers; and (3) Each bank can use a single pool of capital to absorb losses from all risks to which the institution is exposed. In combination these assumptions are founded on the principle that a bank is one single, seamless, integrated entity.

In fact, these assumptions have become less and less valid in the 1980s because of changes in law, regulation, competition, and technology. Thus, the soundness of the traditional model has been seriously undermined.

To understand what has happened, we need to understand each of the underlying assumptions in greater detail. First, let us see how valid they were, and how profitable the model they supported was, from the period after the Second World War to the 1970s.

STABLE, SHARED, NET INTEREST MARGIN

Most banks, even today, employ a pooled funds concept. Essentially, they look at a single net interest revenue number that subtracts interest paid from interest earned. The net interest revenue number for the industry as a whole has historically averaged a little more than 3 percent of all assets (or a little more than 4.5 percent of loans). Through the 1970s net interest

EXHIBIT 1–1
Conceptual Model of a Bank

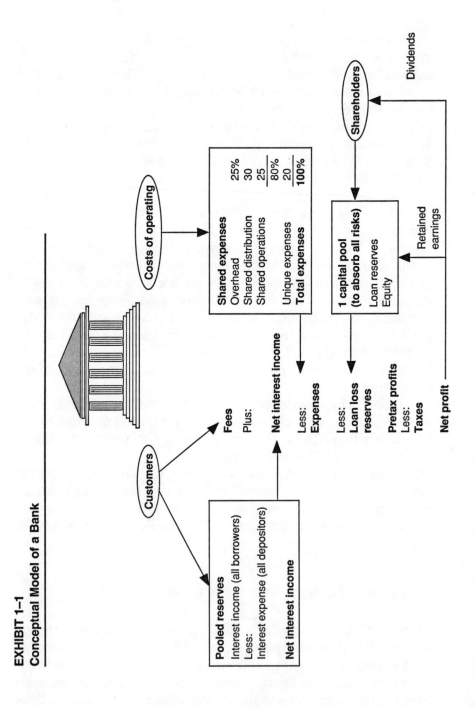

revenue dwarfed other sources of revenue. For example, in 1979 commercial bank net interest income was $57 billion, while total fee income and other sources of revenue totaled only $17 billion. In 1986 net interest income for the industry was $95 billion, while total other revenues were $36 billion.

As you look at the net interest margin numbers for the commercial banking industry in the postwar era (through the 1970s), you are struck by how stable and consistent they appear to be (Exhibit 1-2). This pattern held even in the 1970s, despite the fact that interest rates and economic conditions fluctuated dramatically. For example, the average annual federal funds rate went from 7 percent, down to 4.5, up to 9, down to 5, and then up to over 12 percent during the 1970s. Moreover, net interest margin held nationwide, even though interest rates were dramatically different in different regions of the country for most of the postwar period. For example, in some years in the 1970s, the interest rate on an unsecured consumer loan

EXHIBIT 1–2
Net Interest Margin,* for Insured Commercial Banks, 1970–1980

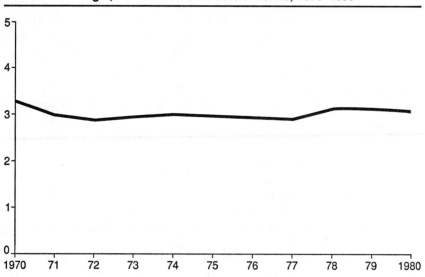

*Net interest income as a percentage of average total assets, not adjusted to taxable equivalent basis.

Source: FDIC

could be as low as 9 percent in one market (Boston) but, at the same time, as high as 15 percent in another market (San Francisco). These differences in pricing were not mysterious. They stemmed from oligopolistic pricing. In effect, each local oligopoly charged borrowers whatever rates were needed in the local market to enable all of the players to maintain their stable net interest margin. These rates were not set by direct collusion; rather, bankers chose to follow local market leaders and compete on service rather than price.

The only truly national marketplace in the postwar era was the large corporate loan market. In this market the industry also used a single price—the prime rate—as the base rate for pricing all corporate loans. So in this market the oligopoly operated on the national, rather than the local, level.

Of course, oligopolies only work where competition is limited to a few players, but the combination of deposit and geographic regulation did that.

SHARED SPENDING PRACTICES

The common pool of net interest income was then used to cover all noninterest expenses. Historically, operating expenses such as salaries and occupancy were dwarfed by interest expenses, but this is becoming less and less true. For example, in 1980 total operating expenses for the commercial banking industry were only 28 percent of total expenses (including interest) of $167 billion. As we will see later, by the end of 1986 operating expenses were 39 percent (i.e., $90 billion) out of total expenses (including interest) of $233 billion.

Another more important historical feature of noninterest expenses is that they have been only loosely linked to revenues. This is to be expected under oligopolistic pricing; in an oligopoly, pricing is determined not by price (and cost) competition, but rather by what the market will bear.

Whenever we at McKinsey have analyzed noninterest expenses in an individual bank, we have seen that the links to revenues are loose indeed. Typically, we find that some 20 to 30 percent of expenses are for pure overhead (i.e., expenses that contribute neither to attracting nor to serving customers); this is not just corporate level overhead, but includes staff support of all levels of bank management. Another 20 to 25 percent are for shared processing and systems expenses. An additional 20 to 30 percent are for shared distribution expenses, including branches. Only the remaining 15 to 20 percent can be attributed to bringing in specific customers and delivering discrete services.

One of the essential features of an oligopoly is that most participants in the industry spend money not to make themselves stand out but rather to prevent competitors from differentiating themselves. Since the members of the oligopoly charge essentially the same prices, they compete based on service and convenience. Therefore, throughout the 1960s and 1970s, bank after bank invested its discretionary funds in nearly identical, service-driven strategies.

The main differences were between kinds of banks—that is, between money center, regional, and community banks. Within each category banks tended to be remarkably similar. Money center banks in New York, Chicago, or San Francisco looked much the same. So did regional banks in Atlanta, Denver, Dallas, or Detroit—as did community banks in New Haven, Omaha, or Greensboro. The same regulation, in the same type of city, resulted in the same type of bank.

SAME CAPITAL POOL

The final assumption that underlies the bundled banking model is explicitly grounded in regulation. The regulation says that each bank should have a single pool of capital that is sufficient to absorb all operating risks. These include credit risks, interest rate risks, earnings risks, and payment risks.

Regulators used capital requirements to ensure that the system was safe and that depositors were well protected. Capital requirements in the 1970s were allowed to vary by the size of the institution; large banks with larger, better diversified loan portfolios were allowed higher leverage than smaller banks. Within a size class, however, requirements were uniform. This made sense because, within a class, the difference between the banks with the highest charge-off rates and those with the lowest charge-off rates was relatively small. (Charge-off rates are rates at which loans are written off as a percentage of loss.) By and large, the industry took very little real credit risk during this period, and it was also only marginally exposed to interest-rate risks (as a whole, the industry's interest-sensitive assets were equal to its interest-sensitive liabilities), payment risks, or other risks.

Thus, by any measure, the banking system in the postwar era was overcapitalized. With loan charge-offs averaging less than .25 percent of assets and with equity capital and reserves averaging approximately 7 percent of assets (that is, over 25 times larger than average charge-offs), there was never a doubt that the industry had enough capital to absorb all loan losses. Indeed, over the 30-year period from 1944 to 1974, only 112 banks failed—and most of those failed because of fraud, not excessive risk taking. In comparison, in 1986 alone 140 banks failed. Throughout this entire period the reserves of the FDIC grew steadily, since deposit insurance premiums greatly exceeded claims upon FDIC reserves from failed banks.

THE BOTTOM LINE

The industry was very profitable in the postwar era. In one particularly profitable year, 1959, its pretax net profits equaled 35 percent of its gross revenues. As a point of reference, in 1986 the industry's pretax net profits equaled only 6 percent of its gross revenues. Through the first three quarters of 1987, the industry actually lost money (thanks to loan loss provisioning for loans to developing countries).

Returns on equity were reasonable. They averaged from 11 to 14 percent a year, after tax, while the average inflation rate was under 3 percent a year until the 1970s. Moreover, the returns were relatively uniform from bank to bank. In 1970, for example, among the 20 largest banks in the country, the best had a return on equity of 13.9 percent, and the worst had a return on equity of 10.2 percent. Bank stocks traded like utilities. Investors expected slow, steady growth and dependable dividends.

Underpinning this profitable business system was the ability to pass on costs to customers, as utilities can. While there was service competition, there was little price competition. If the industry overbranched, costs would be passed along to customers. If regulators required the industry to be overcapitalized, the costs of that capital would again be borne by customers. And as long as the customers had no choice, they went along with the system.

CHAPTER 2

THE ASSUMPTIONS
BREAK DOWN

As the 1970s were coming to a close, depository institutions were extraordinarily profitable. It appeared that our financial system had never been sounder. Yet underneath this appearance of good health, the profitability and stability of the industry were weakening. This was because profitability and stability had always come at the expense of the industry's better customers, who had been subsidizing both the banks and other customers. When these better customers began to leave the system because they had better choices, the industry's foundations began to crack.

DETERIORATION OF
THE CUSTOMER SUBSIDY

The bundled model had worked for so many years because regulation had entrapped for the banks two groups of customers who paid much more for banking services than was justified by the cost of providing those services. In particular, large depositors in both commercial banks and thrifts were not paid the full value for their deposits because of interest rate restrictions, and high-quality corporate borrowers paid commercial banks much more for their loans than their risks would justify. In fact, these customers, who were relatively few in number, not only paid for the vast bulk of the costs of running the entire system, but effectively subsidized other customers as well. For example, small deposit accounts cost the bank more to operate than the value to the bank of the deposits held in them.

In aggregate, the total subsidy became enormous during the late 1970s, as interest rates on loans soared while regulation limited the amount of interest banks could pay on deposits. For example, we estimate that in 1979 depositors in the commercial banking industry alone contributed a subsidy of over $30 billion. (This is the difference between the interest paid on commercial bank deposits under the regulatory ceilings and the value of those deposits at the then prevailing money market rates. See Exhibit 2–1.) In comparison, the commercial banking industry's total pretax profits in that year were only $18 billion.

During the late 1970s McKinsey & Company performed— for its banking clients—a number of economic diagnostics of the depositors of different-sized banks in different parts of the country. Typically, we found that among every customer set examined, approximately 70 to 80 percent of the contribution to profit came from approximately 15 to 25 percent of the customer base. In other words, the profitability and stability of the entire

EXHIBIT 2–1
Value of Deposits above Regulated Ceilings*

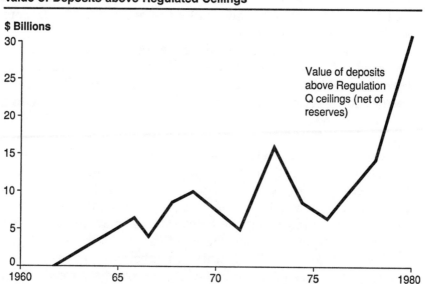

*Includes only the impact of Regulation Q on checking and savings accounts; does not include the impact on time deposits.

Sources: FDIC; McKinsey estimates.

system was provided by a small fraction of total customers. Most often these customers were in three segments: the elderly, the upscale consumer, and corporations of all sizes.

The deposit and lending subsidies fed each other. Because of the enormous deposit subsidy—and the fact that regulation forced most of the funds in the economy to flow through the depository institutions—bankers could afford to be conservative in the credit risks they took. The bargaining power was in their hands. A strong, conservative credit culture existed at most banks in the 1970s. As a result, credit losses were minimal. For example, from 1976 to 1979, the $4 billion of average annual write-offs that prevailed in the commercial banking industry was about .5 percent of loans (about .3 percent of assets). These losses were up substantially from the 1960s—when charge-offs averaged less than .25 percent of loans—but were still not large enough to strain the industry.

This bargaining power, in turn, was used to extract large profits from high-quality corporate borrowers. Often the profits were in the form of large compensating deposit balances, which were protected by regulation. This cross-subsidy enabled bankers to keep actual lending rates relatively low, which made it difficult for nonbank lenders like finance companies to compete for high-quality borrowers.

In the individual market deposits also subsidized loans of two kinds. The first was new loans granted at low rates that were mandated by the usury laws in many states. The second was old, low fixed-rate loans made in the early 1970s that banks and thrifts were unable to reprice as rates soared in the late 1970s.

In effect, banks were passing excess revenues from one set of customers (depositors) through to another set of customers (borrowers). But most bankers did not look at it that way. From their point of view, based on the pooled funds concept, they were simply maintaining their net interest margin. They were relatively indifferent to the source of that margin.

By the late 1970s the traditional subsidies were beginning to disappear. Some of the industry's best customers were becoming dissatisfied with the low value they were receiving for their deposits and the high price they were paying for credit. Those contributing the lion's share of the subsidy became more sophisticated and began leaving the banking system. A process called *disintermediation* then, and *securitization* today, was at work. Regulation had not changed. But nonbanks, primarily securities firms, saw an opportunity to provide value-conscious customers with services these customers needed at a price that was lower than they were paying to banks but was still profitable to the nonbanks, on a product-by-product basis. Unbundled, value-based competition had begun.

On the deposit side, investment management companies began to offer money market funds. To a depositor these funds essentially offered interest-bearing accounts with check writing privileges. They were the functional equivalent of an interest-bearing checking account (although bank regulators ruled that these funds were not checking accounts in the mid-1970s). In the late 1970s, as interest rates rose, large depositors found that they could shift money out of deposit accounts into money market accounts and earn much higher interest (e.g., 12 to 13 percent versus a passbook savings rate of 5.5 or a checking account rate of zero). In other words, sophisticated depositors were recapturing the subsidy for themselves. From a standing start in 1974, money market funds grew to nearly $80 billion in outstandings by the end of 1979. These funds were then invested either in Treasury bills, commercial paper, or large certificates of deposit (which were exempt from the interest rate ceilings).

On the lending side large, high-quality corporate borrowers were discovering at the same time that they could raise money more cheaply in the commercial paper market than they could from banks. Money center banks in 1978 needed at least a 1.5 percent spread over their marginal cost of funds on loans to cover: (1) their cost of equity for regulatory-mandated capital requirements, which in 1978 averaged about .8 percent (today, because capital requirements are higher, it is about 1 percent)*;

---

*The calculations for cost of equity are complex. Determining the required return on equity involves calculation of risk-free return, plus expected earnings growth, plus earnings risk with a given capital structure. In principle, the cost of equity should be the return on equity required to get market value of a company's stock to equal its book value. During the late 1970s this was from 14 to 16 percent. After calculating an estimated cost of equity for industry, we then converted the required return on equity into a spread equivalent.

(2) their FDIC insurance and reserves, which normally cost roughly .3 percent; and (3) their direct operating expenses (loan officers, loan processing, estimated loan losses, etc.) of about .4 percent. At the time banks were charging substantially more than these costs by (1) requiring compensating balances worth roughly 1 percent of outstanding loans and in addition (2) charging at least the "prime" rate for each loan, which brought in an additional 1 percent margin (Exhibit 2–2). This means banks were earning returns on equity of well over 30 percent when their costs of equity were about 16 percent or an "excess" return on equity of over 14 percent.

But large corporate customers learned in the late 1970s that with the aid of the securities industry, they could save at least 1 percent on their borrowings by simply issuing commercial paper, or short-term promissory notes, either on their own

EXHIBIT 2–2
Economics of Large Corporate Lending for Money Center Bank, 1978 (basis points over marginal cost of funds)

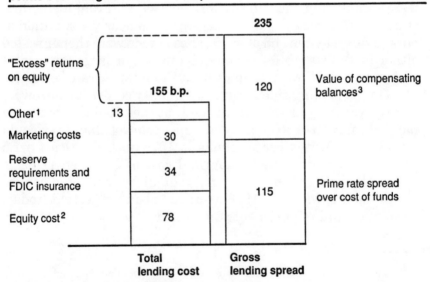

[1]Includes estimated loan losses and asset drag.
[2]Assumes 16 percent ROE required by market, effective tax rate of 40 percent, and leverage of 24X.
[3]Assumed to be 15 percent of outstanding loan.

or with low-cost backup support provided by commercial banks. Throughout the 1970s a huge volume of this sort of commercial paper was issued. By 1979 some $90 billion was outstanding.

Thus, the commercial banking industry began losing the deposit and loan business of its most profitable customers, who moved to institutions that offered better value. All banks and thrifts were affected by the loss of the upscale and elderly depositors. The money center banks were the most affected by the loss of the large corporate customers, who were both large depositors and large borrowers.

BANKING SYSTEM RESPONSE

Banks responded to the loss of customers by spending more than ever before to attract them back. Since banks in the 1970s were prevented by regulation from paying depositors more, and were unwilling to price loans to corporations below the prime rate, they tried to compete by adding services (such as more branches and more automated tellers for individuals, or more tailored cash management services for corporations). They also tried to expand by adding customers to replace the ones they were losing.

These expansion strategies were expensive. From 1976 to 1979 the banking industry's noninterest expenses grew at a compounded rate of 14 percent (from $28 billion in 1976 to $41 billion in 1979). And once one bank started spending, others had to follow simply to prevent any real differentiation in capability. To make matters worse, high inflation rates were driving costs up further.

The banks were working hard, and they were spending hard. But they weren't really strengthening their long-term position. They had increased the *amount* they spent but had not changed their *patterns* of spending to reflect the fact that now their most attractive customers were beginning to look for value on a product-by-product basis. These aggressive expansion strategies were plagued by four serious flaws.

1. *They assumed, falsely, that all spending could be covered by price increases.* In the old oligopoly banks had been able to pass all costs along to customers. Managers spent what they felt they had to and recovered costs simply by allocating them against services, which were then built into prices. The central assumption was that all spending was justified and that all spending should be allocated to whatever products had sufficient margin to absorb the allocation. Thus, allocations had more to do with ability to pay than with economic reality. When customers who were bearing an excessive share of the burden were offered alternatives at better prices, however, the banks lost their ability to pass on costs without losing more customers.

In the late 1970s large individual depositors and corporations were still contributing the lion's share of bank revenues, and they were bearing an ever larger burden of the operating costs for the services used by everyone else (e.g., small depositors, individual borrowers). Since this profitable customer base was shrinking, such subsidy could not go on much longer.

2. *They diffused spending over the whole customer base, rather than focusing on customers the system needed to retain.* Historically, 80 percent of a bank's costs had been unattributable to any specific product or service; the same pattern applied to additional investment. Thus, for example, while money was spent to better serve *depositors in general,* no attempt was made to ensure that the elderly and upscale depositors who were providing what was left of the subsidy felt themselves well served by the improvements.

At times the diffused nature of the investment itself created problems. For example, in search of economies of scale, banks often built very large, shared, automated systems that required computers with enormous power to serve all of the bank's customers for a given product. But they soon found that the needs of individual customers are very different and that it is often very difficult to design a single large system that cost-effectively meets the needs of all users. Invariably, this situation causes compromises on service to all users. For example, the high-volume user may want to minimize costs and may want no-frills service, while the low-volume user may be willing to pay a very high per-item cost and want extra services. If the system is designed for the "average" customer, neither the high- nor the low-volume user will be well served.

Moreover, once an enormous serve-everybody system is built, it often requires significant, continuing modification. In many cases the continuing costs of modification quickly add up to more than the economies of scale the larger system is supposed to yield. More importantly, despite efforts to fix the system after the fact, the repair efforts are never fully successful, and service to customers is seldom satisfactory.

3. *They pursued very similar strategies that because they were parallel, tended to cancel each other out.* In most oligopolies participants work hard to prevent differentiation. Banks operated on the same principle. However, as player after player in the 1970s decided to become more competitive, the costs of trying to maintain parity escalated.

Most of these head-to-head strategies stressed simple expansion. For example, in the late 1970s, many regional banks set up New York and London offices, even though most lacked a customer base, or competitive advantages, or even a strategy for making money on those investments. As long as the additional expense could be covered by cross-subsidies from other customers, managers did not ask about the potential returns on the investment in expansion.

Similarly, bank after bank invested in the same services: networks of automated teller machines, interstate loan production offices, expanded cash management services, international departments, credit cards, and so forth. Only a few of these investments paid for themselves. (Although many today find it hard to believe, bank credit cards were enormous money losers until the 1980s.)

Thus, most of the actions banks took to retain customers left them with neither value nor cost advantages, although they did add to overhead.

4. *They increased the complexity of the bank, which required an expanded, expensive corporate staff.* Many banks now have large functional departments that report to the chief executive office. Some banks have hundreds of corporate-level staff people in personnel, economics, control, systems, marketing, credit administration, management information, and so forth. What is more, as the banks have grown, they have added layer after administrative layer of managers. At each layer, each manager has wanted his or her own staff to control and direct. And true to Parkinson's Law, all of these layers of staff have spent so much time communicating and meeting that more and more staff have been required just to keep up with the growth in paperwork.

Essentially, staffs proliferated because the game had changed, but banks were still playing by the old rules. Banks were looking at their overall net interest margin (which obscured the cross-subsidy of customers and products) and spending of the overall bank (rather than specific products). Nonbank competitors—and increasingly, customers—were thinking in terms of individual product economics and value. Banks had, and have, a structural disadvantage here. Their shared cost structure prevents them from thinking in customer-specific or product-specific terms.

Because spending and revenues are seldom directly linked, management discretion determines most spending—and management seems to see a need for a relatively high level of overhead (in the range of 20 to 30 percent of total noninterest expenses, as mentioned in Chapter 1). Compared to their value-driven competitors, banks spend too much to deliver too little value to customers. What is worse, without a means of understanding where spending adds value, banks often invest revenues from sound products in losers.

By the end of the 1970s most bankers knew that if they continued to lose profitable customers they would be in trouble. And to these bankers other banks' customers seemed increasingly attractive. As a result, bank after bank began to talk about competing more aggressively. And to these aggressive bankers, the regulations that had once protected the industry now seemed to be barriers that were restricting their own profits and opportunities for growth.

Increasingly, these newly aggressive bankers explored ways to get around regulation (particularly geographic regulation). They tended to focus on opportunities where local banks were taking advantage of their customers. In particular, they began to focus on such markets as mid-sized corporations and wealthy individuals. Competition began to spread.

THE VULNERABILITY OF THE BOTTOM LINE

While most bankers understood that they needed to compete more aggressively, precious few understood that they needed to change their approach. The old view continued to prevail because the industry's numbers were still strong.

From 1976 to 1979 the pretax return on the industry's assets increased from about .88 percent to 1.13 percent. The source of this change was a huge increase in the net interest margin as a percentage of assets (+.22 percent). The primary reason for this increase was that the high interest rates then prevailing served to increase the amount of the subsidy being earned from the remaining captive depositors (i.e., those who had not yet moved to money market accounts). From 1976 to 1979 the value of the deposit subsidy on checking and savings accounts went from about $8 billion to $30 billion a year. Moreover, fees as a percentage of assets went up modestly (.04 percent), and the loan loss provision as a percentage of assets actually shrank as a percentage of assets (.09 percent). Only expense growth as a percentage of assets (−.10 percent) indicated the problems that lay ahead. But the earnings, based upon an unsustainable deposit subsidy, were in trouble, because the force of competition had been unleashed.

CHAPTER 3

OLIGOPOLY TO OVERCAPACITY

By 1982 the volume of money market funds had grown to over $200 billion, from a base of under $10 billion four years earlier. Since the bulk of these funds came from bank deposits, the banking and thrift industries were clearly losing their franchise. This was adding insult to injury for the thrifts, which had suffered so badly from high interest rates in 1980 and 1981 that 28 percent of them were either liquidated or merged into stronger institutions from 1980 to 1984.

The two industries, which had rarely agreed upon anything for most of their history, then united to help push through the Garn–St. Germain Act of 1982. This act gave depository institutions power to compete for funds based upon price—both against nonbanks and against each other. With hindsight it is easy to see that the freedom of competition that was hailed at the time was seriously flawed.

The problem was that regulation still prevented the natural consequences of competition—that is, the survival of only the fittest—from taking place. Thus, the failures were protected at the great expense of the skilled institutions in both industries.

DEREGULATION INCREASES BANK AND THRIFT POWER TO COMPETE

The Garn–St. Germain Act had two main features. First, it achieved deposit deregulation, which had been scheduled for completion in 1986, virtually overnight. Now both commercial banks and thrifts could bid for the deposits they had lost. Second, the act attempted to revitalize the thrift industry by expanding its charter. Now thrifts could make many more consumer loans than had been permitted before, as well as lend to businesses and offer demand deposit accounts for the first time. To outside observers thrifts began to look very much like commercial banks.

But the regulators did not seem to see it that way; at least, there was no real attempt to unify or even coordinate the regulation of the two industries. The commercial banks and mutual savings banks continued to be overseen by the FDIC, the Comptroller of the Currency, and the Federal Reserve. The savings and loans (S&Ls) continued to be overseen by the FSLIC and the Federal Home Loan Bank Board.

The attitudes of the two groups of regulators also seemed to differ. The S&L regulators took a laissez-faire approach that gave each S&L institution almost complete autonomy over lending the federally insured deposits it raised. The S&L regulators had little choice; the staffing and skills of the FSLIC and the Federal Home Loan Bank Board were woefully inadequate even to monitor effectively the expanded activities of the S&L industry. The commercial bank and mutual savings bank regulators were much more active, managing not by exception but through strict enforcement of their standards. There is no mystery why, as we will see in Chapter 5, the commercial banking industry is now in much better financial shape than the thrifts.

FEW COMPETITORS ADD UNIQUE VALUE

Banks and thrifts alike fought hard to reestablish their franchises and win new business using their new powers. When they had to, they competed on price—trimming their margins and giving up their traditional customer subsidies. When they could, they kept their prices up and competed based on service, terms, and availability. Some players did very well; others suffered economically but stayed profitable; the rest languished. Before we look at exactly what they did, let us remember some basic truths about what they should have been trying to do.

As Adam Smith observed 200 years ago, the winners in a competitive environment will be the companies that provide the best products, at the lowest prices, to their customers. Their fundamental profit strength will come from adding value to customers relative to competition. The amount of value added can be increased either by making the services more valuable to customers or by managing resources more effectively and efficiently to reduce cost.

Some observers, including myself, would argue that it is more difficult to add distinctively high value in banking than in most industries. There are several reasons for this. First, due largely to regulation, the banking industry is filled with institutions that have relatively similar capabilities, and some of the industry's most important products are virtual commodities (for example, unsecured lines of credit). Second, it is more difficult in banking than in manufacturing or consumer goods industries for managers to get the kind of financial information they need to make sound economic decisions. Primarily, this is because the shared cost structure requires thousands upon thousands of allocations just to construct financial statements, and many of these allocations lack any economic reality. Third, this same shared cost structure prevents any manager below the chief executive from being able to control directly all of the resources and knowledge needed to add maximum value. Fourth, because the business had been a comfortable oligopoly since the Second World War, few banks had bothered to develop the strategic or business skills they need to understand which customers will reward greater value with higher margins or how to deliver value to those customers cost effectively.

Despite such handicaps, some banks and thrifts rose to the challenge and implemented value-added strategies. In so doing, they created enormous opportunities for themselves—since the markets for financial services were very large and growing, since even the largest institutions had only a fraction of the total market, and since much share was held by banks that added relatively little value.

Among the commercial banks there were successes for institutions of all sizes. What these had in common was an understanding of the unique strengths they possessed and the ability to move fast to translate these strengths into value to the customer—without risk to themselves.

Among the money centers Citicorp was a clear leader. Citicorp used its early experience in credit cards and its sheer spending scale to build a huge consumer loan franchise. It was one of the first institutions to compete for lending based on terms and availability, and it could do so more safely than most because it had gotten burned early (in the 1970s) and learned from its mistakes. By the 1980s Citicorp could distinguish the good consumer credits from the bad ones very well.

Bankers Trust took a different tack; it restructured its business by shedding its consumer operations and by concentrating on corporate finance, investment banking, and trading activities to the extent permitted by regulation. For example, in order to compete more effectively against commercial paper, Bankers Trust pioneered the loan sales market, thus maintaining its customer relationships without retaining assets with heavy capital costs. In fact, this was one of the first commercial bank entries into securitization. Bankers Trust also skimmed the leveraged-buyout (LBO) market early, when risk was minimal and returns were still high. Followers, of course, encountered very different conditions.

At the regional level we saw such holding companies as NCNB and BancOne make acquisitions and then rationalize their operations, cutting out back room costs. These holding companies retained the customers they had acquired but cut out capacity and thereby achieved scale economies.

Another regional, State Street Bank, saw a unique advantage in its long-standing relationship with the mutual funds industry. It built a profitable business on the defection of depositors to money market mutual funds by providing check cashing and custodial services to the funds.

There were numerous successes, too, at the community level. The New Canaan Bank and Trust, in my own home town of New Canaan, Connecticut, is an example of a local bank that won simply by providing superior service in a growing market. Part of its success came by working with bigger banks so it would offer "jumbo" mortgage loans that were too large for its own balance sheet.

The unique, value-added strategies contrasted dramatically with the follower strategies of the majority of commercial banks. Most continued as they had in the late 1970s: expanding geographically, competing in parallel, offering the same kind of value using the same technology to the same, largely undifferentiated, groups of customers, at roughly the same time, and for the same price as everyone else. As they competed and expanded, most were forced to invest heavily in staff support to contain the growing risk as their operations became more complex.

Indeed, as the geographic scope of these banks expanded, as the customer base changed, and as the product line proliferated, the banks became more and more difficult to manage. Most banks responded by simply overlaying the management of this expanded activity on top of a management structure designed for a different, simpler era. The points of coordination multiplied.

How could this increased complexity be managed? Most banks were unprepared for a total restructuring; the shared nature of their cost base made the task gargantuan and dangerous to the core business. As a result, internal staff and consultants (including McKinsey) recommended a variety of management approaches, such as matrix management, that would keep the existing organizational structure and underlying economics intact. In parallel, complex management information systems were designed to assist in the management, and motivation, of employees. But it was a losing battle. Most large banks, except for those with exceptional talent and management capacity, became unmanageable. In some large banks three or four projects were often launched to examine the same issue. Redundant functions multiplied, and accountability became blurred. New costs were added, while the "essential," old cost base remained.

As the large banks struggled with the increasing cost of complexity, many smaller banks struggled with the diseconomies of small size. All were trying to offer the same products, but many smaller banks simply had too little volume to support the costs of "essential" new services, like automated tellers (ATMs) or credit cards. For example, in credit cards a large player could reduce its noninterest operating costs (excluding charge-off and collection costs) to 3 or 4 percent of its credit card loan portfolio. For a small community bank the same costs could be 8 to 10 percent or more.

Thus, in commercial banking we saw a great deal of investment in new capabilities and products but surprisingly little creation of unique value for customers. For example, many banks and thrifts simply added distribution (i.e., branches and ATMs). As a result, the number of branches and ATMs doubled from 1975 to 1986, while the household population grew only by 15 percent.

Some S&Ls (particularly on the West Coast) seemed to understand where they were best prepared to add value. Most of them used their new powers only to build on skills they already had. They retained the same simple business structure they had built through the years, which focused on simply taking deposits and originating mortgages. They grew their business by taking more deposits and investing more in mortgages, while strengthening their treasury skills in an effort to manage the interest rate risk that had hurt them in 1980 and 1981. (So far, these strategies have not been tested in an environment of high interest rates or an inverted yield curve. To date, some of these traditional savings and loans have seemed to offer customers good value, economically.)

Many other S&Ls proceeded with much less caution. Most took full advantage of their new charter powers to add new services, investing heavily to build organizations that began to look much more like commercial banks. But they were entering product areas that were already well served by commercial banks, and few S&Ls had unique skills in offering these services. Thus, as we will see in Chapter 4, many thrifts competed by taking on more and more credit risk.

Some of these thrifts, which had not recovered from the high interest rates of 1980 and 1981, suffered early profitability problems. Some, in fact, became insolvent and should have been liquidated as early as 1983 or 1984. They were able to remain open by raising deposits—not to make loans or other investments, but rather to pay interest on existing deposits. This type of business was a money maker for Charles Ponzi in Boston from 1919 to 1920, but it is not a long-term winning strategy. Ponzi developed a scheme in which he promised an "investor" high rates on his money (40 percent for 45 days), then borrowed larger sums from later investors, took a cut, and used the remainder to pay the interest on the first money given him. This pyramid scheme yielded high returns to Ponzi until *The Boston Post* exposed him, and he was indicted.

While the struggling thrifts are not as blatant as Ponzi, the principle is the same—only in this case, the guarantor is the federal government, not Charles Ponzi. And this brings us to the fundamental problem in the new competitive environment in which the commercial banks and thrifts were operating: regulation prevented the losers from disappearing, and all players suffered as a result.

REGULATION PREVENTS INDUSTRY SHAKEOUT, CREATING OVERCAPACITY

During the years following Garn–St. Germain things moved fast for banks and thrifts. They regained many of their lost depositors by offering money market accounts that involved an irresistible combination of high rates, high liquidity, government insurance, and branch-based service. The deposits in such accounts grew from nothing to nearly $600 billion between 1982 and 1986 (Exhibit 3–1). That stopped the growth of money market mutual funds. But the banks and thrifts had lost their deposit subsidy forever—partly because they were now paying more for the deposits they had regained and partly because even the remaining demand and savings deposits became less valuable as interest rates fell. In the commercial banking industry the value of the deposit subsidy fell from some $30 billion in 1979, to less than $15 billion in 1983, to nearly zero by 1986 (in fact, in 1986 passbook rates on savings in some cases exceeded the rates paid on money market accounts).

Consequently, banks started to look for more profits in lending businesses—and found them, although not in their traditional high-profit areas. The inroads of securitization, and the increase in competition, made corporate lending more of a buyers' market than ever. The prime rate pricing system

EXHIBIT 3–1
Money Market Funds vs. Money Market Deposit Accounts

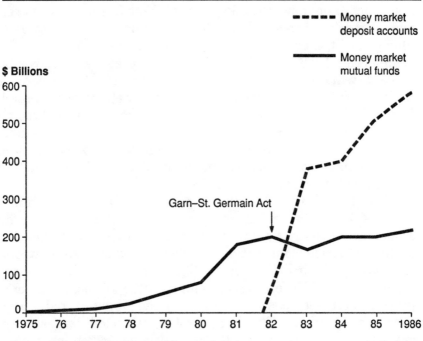

Sources: Federal Reserve; Investment Company Institute

broke down completely, and prime became a rate used essentially only for smaller borrowers. Banks started pricing corporate loans directly off their marginal cost of funds. As the volume of deposits in short-term money market accounts soared, there was a shortage of high-quality, floating-rate assets. As a result, spreads declined rapidly on all loans to large and mid-sized corporations. By 1984 most banks were getting only .25 percent over their marginal cost of funds (that is, .25 percent over the incremental costs of raising the bank's most expensive deposits) and less than 1 percent over their marginal cost of funds for loans to mid-sized companies. Since banks in the 1980s need a spread of over 1.5 percent just to cover the cost of equity capital, reserves, and FDIC insurance, incremental large corporate lending was clearly not justified.

Banks found a new cross-customer subsidy, albeit a transient one, in consumer lending. They had dramatically increased consumer loan rates in 1980 and 1981 as they received usury ceiling relief, and now they kept those higher rates as overall money market rates fell. By 1986 consumer lending (particularly credit card lending) became very, very profitable. For example, in 1986 prevailing credit card rates were at over 20 percent, while money market rates were in the 5 to 6 percent range—leaving an enormous 14 percent net interest spread. Even after allowing 7 to 8 percent for charge-offs and operating expenses, the resulting profits were enormous for most banks. There were a few other pockets of profitability for banks, too, where demand was relatively inelastic. These included loans to small businesses and trust services.

But profitability, under competition, is always a double-edged sword. The profits from consumer lending saved the economics of many banks, at least temporarily, but they led to hot nonprice competition in these product areas among the banks. Many offered more liberal terms, such as longer repayment periods or higher loan-to-value ratios. And some players accepted business that carried higher credit risk than was prudent. The high profits attracted larger players who were already in these businesses—such as money center banks, regional banks, life insurance companies, and securities firms—to new, previously local markets. What was even worse for the banks and thrifts, however, was that the profits also attracted specialist and nonbank competitors who could come in under the price umbrella. (These new competitors could offer, for example, consumer credit through dedicated, cost-effective operations.) These institutions—which included finance companies, leasing companies, mutual fund companies, and foreign banks in specialty markets—could still be immensely profitable while offering slightly lower prices to customers. As a result, we are now seeing price competition across the board, even in consumer lending. Moreover, consumer loan losses have been rising rapidly.

Under fully competitive circumstances the situation would sort itself out. The competitors unable to provide value, as Adam Smith defined it, would be driven into bankruptcy, and their capacity would be eliminated from the system, while their customers transferred their business to the surviving players.

This elimination of capacity is essential to maintaining the profitability of the survivors.

Thanks to regulation, however, banks and thrifts that fail are kept in the system. Continental Illinois, Seattle First, and more recently the subsidiaries of the Financial Corporation of America, First City Bancorporation (Houston), and First Republic Bancorporation (Dallas), not to mention a host of smaller banks and thrifts, have all been bailed out, and their capacity has thus remained in the system. From a regulatory viewpoint this makes perfect sense. Bailing out banks and thrifts minimizes the costs (at least in the short term) to the deposit insurance funds. It also, in the case of large commercial banks, protects the nation's payment system.

From an industry economics viewpoint, however, bailouts are harmful. With too much capacity chasing too little business, profitability has suffered in all the financial services. Looking at banks, thrifts, insurance companies, securities companies, and finance companies together, aggregate profits have grown at an annual rate of only about 2.5 percent compounded from 1979 to 1986, while the pretax returns on equity for the aggregate financial services industry fell from about 20 percent to 12 percent. The commercial banking industry suffered a little more than most; from 1979 to 1986 the pretax profits of commercial banking grew only from $17.9 billion to $19 billion (less than 2 percent compounded), while pretax return on equity fell from 19.3 percent to 10.9 percent. Two sectors of the financial services showed improvement, at the expense of the commercial banks. Securities firms took advantage of securitization, as well as a bull equity market, to increase their pretax profitability from an annual rate of $1.7 billion in 1979 to over $8 billion in 1986. And consumer finance companies took advantage of the price umbrella created by banks in the consumer loan market to increase their profits from $1.9 billion in 1979 to nearly $6 billion in 1986, for an increase in pretax return on equity from 15 to 27 percent.

Banks should clearly be worried about overcapacity, but we should all be concerned. The health of the entire financial services sector is threatened. At the end of the day, continued overcapacity will limit the profitability of all players, even those institutions in the most attractive sectors. For example, entering 1988 even the securities industry showed signs of real over-capacity, and consumer finance profitability was threatened by increased price competition for consumer loans. This situation is not surprising given the growth of capacity in the entire financial services industry, as measured by expense and capital growth, from 1981 to 1986 (Exhibits 3–2 and 3–3) greatly outstripped growth in the Gross National Product (GNP).

EXHIBIT 3–2
Growth in Expense Capacity, 1981–1986

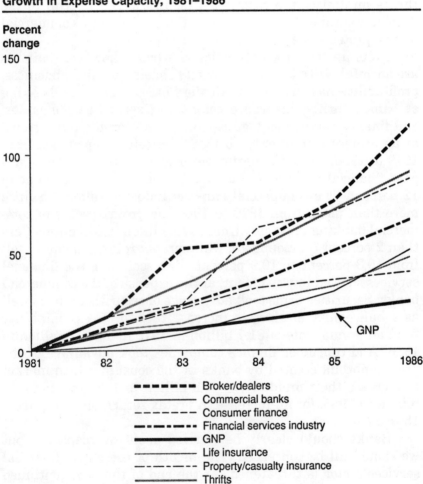

Source: McKinsey analysis

EXHIBIT 3–3
Growth in Capital Capacity, 1981–1986

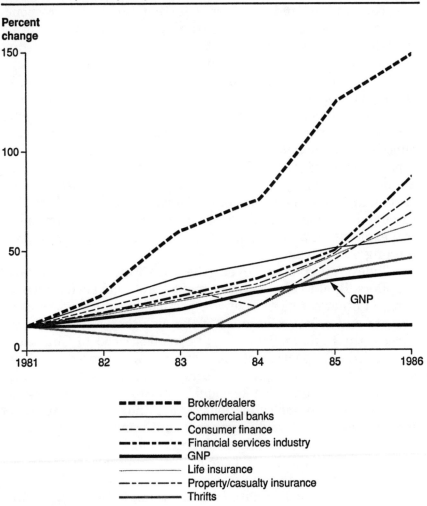

Percent
change

Legend	
▬ ▬ ▬ ▬	Broker/dealers
————	Commercial banks
– – – – –	Consumer finance
▬ ▪ ▬ ▪ ▬ ▪	Financial services industry
▬▬▬▬	GNP
··········	Life insurance
– · – · – ·	Property/casualty insurance
▬▬▬▬	Thrifts

Source: McKinsey analysis

Many industries have been plagued periodically by overcapacity—for example, airlines, chemicals, automobile manufacturers, and oil producers. But few have regulators who keep the capacity of failing participants in the system. Perhaps the best analogy I know of is steel, where governments—particularly in

Europe—subsidize failing competitors. Here again, protective regulation seems misdirected.

The banking industry has a further problem in responding to overcapacity and intensifying competition. In other industries experiencing these twin difficulties, one important response is to disaggregate and restructure integrated suppliers, usually through spin-offs, mergers, joint ventures, or shared production. In this process one complex business system is unbundled and reformed into several simple ones, with each stage in the production function now performed by a cost-effective participant. In the restructuring process redundant capacity is eliminated. We have seen such restructuring in the automobile industry, where even the largest manufacturers use parts manufactured by specialty companies and distribute cars through independent dealers. Similarly, in the petroleum industry, exploration and production is increasingly separated from refining and marketing.

Today all banks, even the smallest, are integrated suppliers. Banks raise deposits, make loans, and perform a wide array of other services. They are particularly difficult to disaggregate and redesign because of the way they have grown up. Indeed, the basic model of a bank (as described in Chapter 1) is founded on a pooled net interest margin, a shared cost base, and a single pool of capital. As competition intensifies and puts pressure on margins, banks should want to eliminate marginal activities and to shed functions where they are inefficient or ineffective—that is, to disaggregate. But bundled costs and revenues make this very difficult. A bank that is particularly good at lending, but relatively poor at gathering deposits, can not shed its deposit gathering operations. Conversely, a bank that is particularly good at gathering deposits, but is poor at finding high-quality borrowers, can not simply shed lending activities and concentrate on deposit gathering. Moreover, bankers have discovered that it would make little economic sense to shed marginal activities, even if they could, because the shared costs and capital that are allocated to divested activities do not disappear with the divestment. In other words, simple divestment only works to reduce revenues, while the expenses and the capital remain.

With profits under pressure bank and thrift managers have generally taken two steps: First, they have tried to reduce spending, and, second, they have attempted to keep up the net interest margin by booking profitable loans. In both areas their methods have been flawed—although it is not clear what other approaches they could have taken within the traditional bank model and regulatory structure to which they are tied.

In their attempts to halt the growth of spending, many bank managers have found themselves hamstrung by the traditional, shared cost structure. Because structure makes only minimal connections between spending and profitability, one can not see what spending contributes most to returns and what spending contributes least. True, allocation formulas are used to force various lines of business to bear their part of each bank's shared cost structure, but we at McKinsey believe that such formulas are usually highly arbitrary and often highly inconsistent. For example, we saw one regional bank in one part of the country whose allocation formula showed that a certain product line was unprofitable, while another regional bank in another part of the country judged the same product line to be profitable, even though the product revenues were the same for the two banks. The difference was in the way that costs, which had only an indirect relation to the product line, were allocated.

Sensing that allocation formulas would not aid them in judicious cost cutting, most bank managers began to cut costs in roughly the same way they had increased them earlier: across the board. This usually meant cutting new discretionary spending on new products, new skills, and so forth—that is, they were cutting the very spending that was most essential. Meanwhile, the existing, entrenched shared cost base that supported the whole structure was rarely challenged. As long as the bank was going to operate on the historic model, this spending was essential.

Despite attempts at economy, costs continued to go up alarmingly, industry wide. Even though inflation had slowed from the 7 percent annual range in the 1970s to the 3 percent range in the 1980s, bank spending continued to surge with increasing competition. It grew at a compounded annual rate of about 14 percent from 1980 through 1986, reaching in that year an annual volume across the commercial banking industry of $90 billion.

There was little to do, under the traditional bank model, but increase business to maintain the net interest margin, even though the margins of high-quality business were falling. In the process, many took risks that should not have been taken. That is the subject of the next chapter.

CHAPTER 4

PROTECTIVE REGULATION
BECOMES OBSOLETE

During the early to mid-1980s some indicators suggested that the U.S. financial services industry in general—and the banking and thrift industries in particular—seemed to be headed down the same path as the worldwide steel industry.

But almost miraculously, net interest revenues still appeared healthy. Despite intensified price competition for large individual depositors and for large corporations, the net interest margin for the commercial banking industry, at least, had not declined much as a percentage of average earning assets through 1986. In fact, the net interest margin as a percentage of assets for the industry in 1986 was only 3.9 percent, which was .2 percent lower than it had been in 1978.

How was this possible? The unfortunate evidence is that many players in both the commercial banking and thrift industries had maintained their net interest margins by lowering their standards and accepting higher levels of both credit and interest rate risk. The results of such practices show only over time. They are beginning to show now, when it is too late to change them. We are also finding now that the regulatory safety nets on which our banking and thrift systems are based are woefully inadequate for setting things right.

In fact, we are beginning to realize that our credit system is breaking down.

I am not referring to the problem of LDC debt from loans to less-developed countries like Brazil and Mexico. That debt is a problem to be sure, particularly to a handful of money center banks, but one that is shared by other banks in other nations and one that is now being addressed. Much progress has been made in recognizing the extent of loan losses to the LDCs and provisioning for them. Indeed, this provisioning is a primary reason why the commercial banking industry lost over $5 billion during the first half of 1987. While additional provisioning may be required, plenty of attention and energy are being applied to the LDC problem loans—at least by the banks. Moreover, it is highly unlikely that banks will repeat their mistakes in lending to these countries. This is not to say that the LDC debt problem is solved; that would require actions by the governments of the industrial world, the banks, and the nations themselves. But while we await the ultimate answer, we are unlikely to see much impact of the LDC debt problem on the U.S. banking system. At the worst, I would expect the forced restructuring of one or more money center banks. Frankly, we have bigger worries elsewhere.

What we should be worrying most about is the breakdown of the domestic credit system, which is being destroyed gradually by the same combination of regulation, partial competition, and overcapacity that I have just described. This is not a problem of judgment, as LDC debt was. It is a problem in the system itself. Unless there are changes in regulations, and in a number of other assumptions on which our credit system is based, many banks and thrifts will suffer more and more as time goes on. And, in time, that suffering will be borne by the citizens of this country.

Let's examine what has been happening to credit quality and why current regulation is now incapable of preserving the soundness of our credit system. Then, in the next chapter, we can consider the likely consequences of allowing the system, and the problems, we now have to continue.

REGULATION ENCOURAGES UNSOUND LENDING

In fact, the regulation that was designed to protect the credit system is now destroying it, because it now defines an industry that is only partially competitive. The underlying government subsidies to all competitors are still in place. All banks and thrifts can back up their deposits (up to $100,000 per depositor) with government insurance. Naturally, under such circumstances, depositors choose where to put their money on the basis of which bank offers the highest interest rate rather than on which one is the soundest.

Too often, however, the highest bidder has been an incompetent commercial bank or thrift. In some cases, S&Ls with less than $100 million in assets in 1982 raised money through brokers and grew to multi-billion-dollar institutions in just a few years. These institutions then started lending aggressively, and the increase in capacity forced lending spreads down.

As they watched capacity grow, many institutions that had been dominated by a conservative credit culture saw their net interest margin threatened. Some reacted by relaxing their quality and lending standards to get the best margins they could. Danger loomed, because while many credit officers in the past had been conservative, many were not particularly skillful.

Banks were forced by the local marketplace to charge a certain interest rate, but they were left to themselves to determine the quality of each risk and the potential loss on each loan. Competition prevented them from using the traditional, conservative standards for acceptable terms and prudent lending limits. New standards had to be developed within each bank, because for most borrowers there are neither ratings nor common information sources that assess the quality of credit or interest rate risks. Setting and following new standards required sophisticated skills in gathering credit information, underwriting credits, perfecting collateral, and collecting delinquent loans. Many banks—and even more thrifts—were unable to build those skills. Indeed, many thrifts that had been handed a blank check in 1982 to underwrite credit with government-guaranteed funds had never had a credit culture of any kind before.

The best, most highly skilled commercial banks underwrote more aggressive credits with only minimal increases in problem credits and charge-offs, although these credits have not yet been tested by a recession. In less skilled commercial banks, on the other hand, bad credits were often accepted without real understanding of the risks. The hungriest (and least prudent) institutions accepted borrowers whose financial condition was so risky that they should have been raising equity instead. In the worst thrifts, finally, there appears to have been not only a lack of skill but fraud and malfeasance as well.

The net result was the low-quality borrowers were able to borrow at rates nearly the same as the good credits were paying. McKinsey's research supports this point and demonstrates that, overall, the commercial banking industry has clearly not been able to charge borrowers for the risk they are taking. For high-risk debt, returns are actually negative if one estimates loan losses accurately. That is, the industry is underwriting uneconomic credit risk. Risk and return are not correlated.

And yet, as I noted in the beginning of this chapter, very few bankers sensed a real problem until recently. In 1986 the economics of most banks, and even many thrifts, still looked good. This is because increased risk taking postpones economic losses—at least for a while. When you assume more credit or interest rate risk, you can bring more income forward (in terms of current interest and front-end fees); if you are wrong, the losses come later.

On the credit risk side it often takes years for loans to go bad: banks are still recognizing losses today from loans extended (and income booked) in the early 1980s.

On the interest-rate risk side losses come only when short-term rates rise. Here we seem to be sitting on another, equally dangerous time bomb. From analysis of the incomplete FDIC figures that exist, we estimate that the commercial banking industry is now mismatching the funding of some $300 billion of assets by borrowing short and lending long. With at least a 4 to 5 percent yield differential between fixed-rate residential mortgage rates and money market account rates in 1987, it has been easy enough for a bank to maintain its net interest margin by taking interest rate bets. Indeed, we believe some $12 billion of income, equal to about 60 percent of the industry's 1986 pretax profits, was due to interest rate betting. Moreover, we believe the thrift industry is taking even more rate risk than that.

Thus, the net interest margin looked healthier than it

really was because it was masked by both unsustainable interest risk taking and understated loan losses. As long as bank managers looked only at the bottom line, they could continue to operate under the illusion that nothing was really wrong, that nothing, really, had changed. They could believe that this, too, would pass and that business as usual, based on the traditional model of the bank, could continue.

WARNING SIGNALS APPEAR

Yet, at least on the credit loss side, there were clear warning signs by the end of 1986. Domestic loan charge-offs had risen to a rate of $17 billion a year (Exhibit 4–1), which was over 1 percent of loans—even though between 1981 and 1986 we had enjoyed a highly stimulative fiscal and monetary policy and

EXHIBIT 4–1
Commercial Bank Net Charge-offs

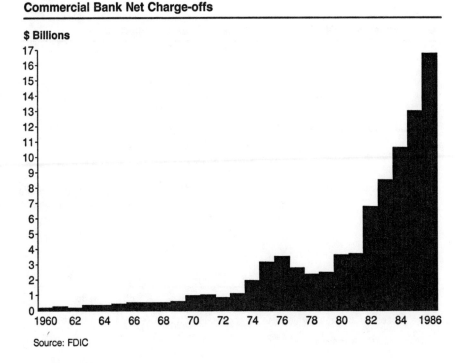

$ Billions

Source: FDIC

an economic boom. In contrast, the postwar average had been under .25 percent of assets.

If we net loan charge-offs against the net interest margin, we begin to see the squeeze we expected on net interest margin. Adjusted for charge-offs, the net interest margin fell steadily from 1982 onward (Exhibit 4–2). Moreover, to the extent that income continued to be front-end loaded as credit standards continued to erode, the actual erosion of net interest margins on a risk-adjusted basis was actually far larger.

At this point it becomes difficult to speak about the problems of either the commercial banking industry or the thrift industry as a whole. There were, and are, credit problems and resulting financial losses that are coming increasingly to light. But they are not industry wide. The quality of the earnings of some, but not all, institutions has deteriorated sharply. Some, but not all, institutions, are losing money. Our figures show that in 1986 (before any LDC debt was written off) 2,500 of the nation's 14,000 commercial banks were losing money. But

EXHIBIT 4–2
Commercial Bank Net Interest Margins and Net Charge-offs*

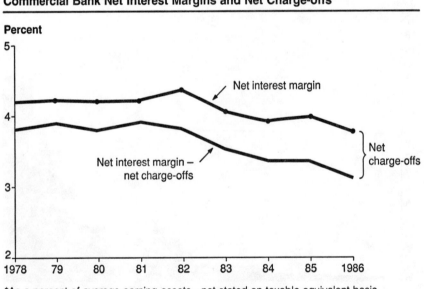

*As a percent of average earning assets—not stated on taxable equivalent basis.

Sources: FDIC; McKinsey analysis

some of our institutions, those that developed the needed skills and implemented value-added strategies, are still doing very well. The dispersion in performance for both banks and thrifts has widened enormously (Exhibits 4–3 and 4–4).

We no longer have an oligopoly with roughly equal levels of skill and roughly equal returns. We have fierce competition with divergent levels of skill and divergent returns. The credit problems have been concentrating in the institutions with the poorest credit underwriting skills which have booked the greatest volume of bad loans. If the credit system were fully competitive, these weak players would never be able to raise deposits and make loans in such volumes. Ultimately, they would fail. But in the system as it operates today, most poorly managed institutions continue to raise funds with the backing of the federal government and turn them into increasingly bad loans.

Let's look at the commercial banking and thrift industries in turn. We will see how bad the credit problem is in each and how concentrated the problem is.

EXHIBIT 4–3
Dispersion of Commercial Bank Earnings

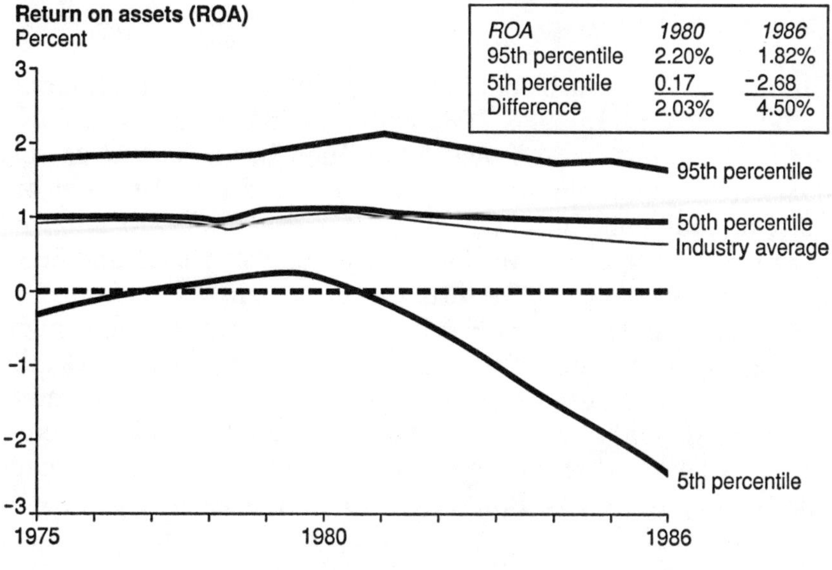

Return on assets (ROA)
Percent

ROA	1980	1986
95th percentile	2.20%	1.82%
5th percentile	0.17	-2.68
Difference	2.03%	4.50%

Sources: Federal Reserve Bulletin; FDIC; McKinsey analysis

EXHIBIT 4–4
Dispersion of Thrift Institution Earnings*

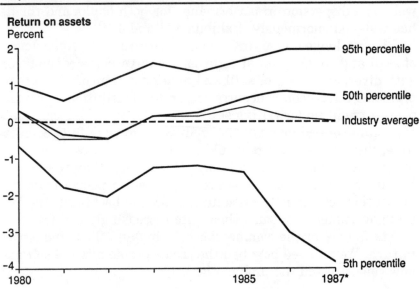

*Annual data for FSLIC-insured institutions; 1987 data are for first quarter (annual rate).

Source: Federal Reserve Bulletin

Commercial Banks

Charge-offs have grown alarmingly in the U.S. commercial banking system. In 1985, 1986 and 1987, the commercial banking industry charged off over $45 billion in almost exclusively domestic debt (banks have made provisions for LDC debt but most of that debt has not yet been charged off). To put that number in perspective, in the 30 years between 1951 and 1980, the industry charged off a total of $28 billion.

Moreover, the reported $45 billion figure probably underestimates the amount of uncollectable loans the banks actually were holding. Most loans are written off based on judgment rather than pure numbers, and banks are understandably reluctant to admit to themselves and the public that they have made bad lending decisions. Bankers have often chosen to be slow to recognize emerging losses, hoping against hope that the loans would get better rather than worse.

The charge-offs are, as we have noted before, concentrated. Further, McKinsey's analysis shows that the banks with the worst charge-off experience are not able to enjoy higher margins as a result of greater risk taking, even in the short term. We have analyzed charge-off statistics for the entire commercial banking industry and have arrayed the industry in deciles from the best to the worst. From this analysis we have found that all banks in each decile earn roughly the same net interest margin as a percentage of earning assets—about 4.6 percent. Thus, there is no additional net interest margin for taking additional credit risk. In fact, when we net out charge-offs, we see that the higher the real credit risk taken in lending, the worse the economics of the bank (Exhibit 4–5). This is in sharp contrast to the bond market, where credit ratings and yields are more closely correlated.

About 11 percent of the commercial banks—1,500 institutions in all—are in very weak financial condition, having suf-

EXHIBIT 4–5
Commercial Bank Net Interest Margin–Charge-offs* by Net Charge-off Rate Deciles (Median Values for 1986)

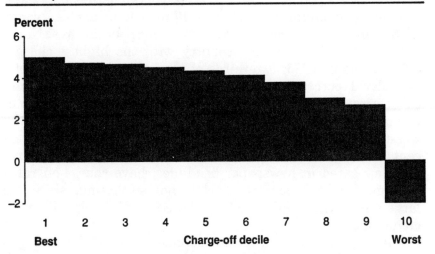

*Stated on a taxable equivalent basis as a percent of average earning assets.

Sources: FDIC; McKinsey analysis

fered much more from charge-offs than their competitors. A bank at the median of our array charges off .8 percent of its loans and leases in any given year; the worst 10 percent wrote off about 6 percent of loans and leases in 1986, while another 10 percent wrote off about 3 percent of loans and leases in that year. Put another way, banks that account for just 8 percent of the industry's assets accounted for 32 percent of its charge-offs in 1986.

Problem banks are concentrated in geographic regions experiencing hard times, and we also see worse charge-offs in banks serving troubled industries, like farming and energy. This is to be expected; it usually takes economic adversity to transform credit risk into loan losses. What might be more surprising is that within these pockets of poor performance, the loan losses are concentrated again. If we examine any subgroup of banks, like farm banks, or other community/local banks, or banks in the West North Central region, we find that most of the members of the group are performing reasonably well and a few (roughly 20 to 30 percent in most cases) are performing badly. For example, it is true that some farm banks are troubled. But 20 percent of farm banks, in terms of assets, account for 54 percent of all the farm banks' charge-offs. Of the remaining community/local banks, 17 percent by assets account for 58 percent of the charge-offs of that group. In the West North Central, the region of the country with the highest charge-off patterns in 1986, two-thirds of the banks have charge-offs of under 1 percent, while the worst 10 percent are charging off at a rate of more than 7 percent of assets. In one group of banks—the nation's 150 largest banks—charge-offs of the worst performers are less extreme. Even the worst 10 percent of these banks, whose names and credit problems have often appeared in newspaper headlines, have charge-off rates averaging only 2 percent. This is not surprising, since the large size of the loan portfolios of these banks helps diversify credit risk.

All this being said, it became clear in 1988 that there is one state, Texas, where the majority of the depository institutions in the state are troubled. Even here, though, the differences in relative trouble, from the best to the worst, is enormous.

Savings and Loans

The S&L industry is weaker overall than commercial banking, but here, too, there are strong institutions as well as weak ones. Roughly 40 percent of the industry is very solvent, with capital ratios approximately equal to commercial bank standards. Another 30 percent, although significantly undercapitalized by commerical bank standards, are nonetheless still technically solvent (that is, they have a positive net worth).

We should view these figures with guarded optimism, however. For one thing, it remains to be seen how many of these solvent thrifts would be so if their bad loans, low interest mortgages, and mortgage-backed securities were marked to market prices. For another, those mortgages and mortgage-backed securities should be a real cause for concern, because they embody so much interest rate risk. Many thrifts hold large amounts of both, which they list on their balance sheets at the price they paid for them. Typically, the thrifts fund these mortgage assets with short-term, interest-rate sensitive deposits. When interest rates go up, the thrifts are hit on both sides of their balance sheets. The market value of their mortgages and mortgage-backed securities goes down, and the price they must pay for their deposits goes up.

How dangerous, exactly, is the interest rate risk exposure of the thrifts? To judge that, consider what occurred between mid-March and mid-April of 1987. Interest rates rose so fast that the principal value of many mortgage-backed securities dropped by 7 percent. Since the thrift industry holds about $135 billion of these securities, that movement reduced the value of the industry's assets by about $10 billion—or 62 percent of the industry's total tangible net worth—in just one month. While some thrifts may have guarded against a portion of this loss by hedging, the actual loss is likely to have been greater, since the value of the thrifts' fixed-rate, whole-mortgage portfolios also declined. Fortunately for all of us, long-term interest rates peaked in October (right before the stock market crash) and have since headed downward (through early 1988). Should rates reverse themselves, we could have enormous losses in the thrift industry.

In the meantime, the industry has plenty of credit-related

problems. Thirty percent of the S&Ls in this country—some 1,000 in number—are already insolvent or are on the verge of becoming insolvent. Since the GAAP (Generally Accepted Accounting Principles) net worth of many thrifts typically includes intangibles (e.g., "goodwill") equal to 3 percent of assets, which may have little or no market value, many of these low net worth thrifts are also actually insolvent on a tangible net worth basis. Even if you count intangibles as real equity, some 13 percent of the thrifts operating in 1986 were insolvent (that is, they had negative GAAP net worths). By the end of 1987 the number had grown to 17 percent.

Why are these thrifts still operating? Because the thrift regulators have, since 1980, permitted thrifts to use accounting practices that artificially inflate the thrifts' regulatory net worth above GAAP conventions. Moreover, thrifts can still raise the cash they need to keep the doors open because of government guarantees. As long as losing thrifts retain these privileges, they will have incentives to make very risky loans and to take huge interest rate gambles, because they have nothing to lose. If the risk taking succeeds, they may be able to generate a positive net worth for their shareholders and continue paying salaries to managers. If the risk taking fails, the only real loser is the FSLIC insurance fund that will have to cover the thrift's inability to repay its depositors. The perverse incentive that arises when an insolvent insured thrift is permitted to continue operating has been summarized by other observers as: "Heads I win, tails FSLIC loses."

The longer insolvent thrifts are permitted to play these losing games, the greater their losses will be. As a result, the negative worth of these operating insolvent thrifts is deteriorating at an accelerating and frightening rate. In 1984 the negative net worth of the average operating insolvent thrift was negative 3.5 percent of assets. Two years later, in 1986, this average negative net worth had grossly deteriorated to negative 8.5 percent. The reason why the net worth of these thrifts is compounding at a negative rate is that these are the institutions that are raising deposits just to stay in business (i.e., paying interest on existing deposits and funding operating losses) as opposed to making new loans.

REGULATORY SAFETY NETS
ARE BREAKING DOWN

A depositor might ask why he should be concerned about these losses. After all, isn't there government insurance to bail out failed institutions and keep the system sound? Aren't there regulatory requirements that force banks and thrifts to reserve against losses? The answer is that there is and there are, but that, again, these safeguards are designed for a system in which everyone plays the same game, with roughly the same returns. Unfortunately, that system is long gone. Let's look at the regulation first and then consider how inadequate it is to cope with the kind of skewed performance we see today in the commercial banking and thrift industries.

The existing credit system provides for several layers of coverage that shield depositors from credit losses. First, a loan that is recognized as uncollectable is charged off against reserves. If reserves are felt to be insufficient to cover all losses, they are raised by increasing the loan loss provision. This action reduces earnings. If earnings are insufficient, then the necessary increases in the provision create losses. If losses occur enough years in a row, the institution runs out of capital and becomes insolvent. Federal deposit insurance funds are designed to be a last layer of protection for the depositors who have put their funds in such institutions.

Commercial bank regulators have historically required U.S. commercial banks to keep a combination of loan loss reserves and equity capital of roughly 6 percent of assets (in practice, the target number is closer to 7 percent). The capital guideline is a rule of thumb approximation of the capital needed for the "average" loan and the "average" bank. This single pool of capital is supposed to provide cross-subsidized protection against *all* risks. First, it includes specific reserves for credit losses. Second, it includes substantial equity capital to protect against catastrophic loan losses and other unspecified risks, including interest rate risk and prepayment risk. These reserves and equity capital are supposed to be sufficient to protect depositors against inadequate diversification of credit risk. Regulators believe most banks are too small, serve too narrow a range of customers, or are too geographically concentrated to have safely diversified portfolios; this belief causes regulators to require more capital.

In any case, this level of capital requirement would seem to be more than enough, in aggregate, to cover loan losses, since historically most banks have had very low levels of charge-offs. The average commercial bank has charged off an average of about one-half of 1 percent of its average assets over the last five years. That means the average bank has been keeping well over 15 times its average charge-offs in loan loss reserves and equity capital.

In fact, despite the growth of charge-offs, the industry could still cover them easily if all its earnings, loan loss reserves, and capital were available to absorb all its expected losses. In 1986 the almost 14,000 commercial banks in this country earned a total of $17 billion pretax and held roughly $21 billion in loan loss reserves and $200 billion in capital. Thus, the total available protection was about 15 times charge-offs—*if* all this protection were available to absorb losses. However, the capital and reserves of the strongest banks are not available to absorb the losses of the weakest.

The S&L regulators have been more lenient. Seeing that thrifts had less capital, thrift regulators pragmatically lowered their de facto capital requirements. Thrift accounting, being the *Alice in Wonderland* game that it is, makes it very difficult to compute numbers that enable us to compare the thrift industry with commercial banks. Nevertheless, it is possible to note that at the end of 1986 the tangible net worth of the S&L industry was only about 1.5 percent of its assets. In contrast, the tangible net worth of the commercial banking industry was roughly 6 percent of its assets.

To sum up, the traditional regulatory system is flawed on several counts. First, it assumes that depository institutions will avoid uneconomic credit risk. But the reality is that weak players faced with a squeeze on margins will gamble, especially if they have nothing to lose. This tendency makes the regulatory task impossible; regulators can not second-guess credit decisions before the loans are made.

Second, the traditional regulatory system implicitly assumes that banks can charge sufficient spreads to cover their costs. However, the combination of competition and regulatory protection of failing institutions is leading to overcapacity which in turn is making it difficult for most participants to earn satisfactory profits.

The central flaw of the traditional regulatory system is that it depends on having more than enough capital in each bank (or thrift) to ensure that bank equity holders rather than the deposit insurance funds absorb all losses. As we have seen, however, capital levels that are more than adequate for the "average" bank are in fact grossly inadequate for an alarmingly large number of institutions with alarmingly poor performance. Further, they are unreasonably high for the many banks with high-quality, broadly diversified loan portfolios.

At the end of the day, the federal deposit insurance funds are the losers—as long as they hold out. When they fail, it is hard to see how all of us taxpayers can avoid being losers, in turn. That day is not as far away as some people, particularly in Washington, seem to hope it is.

CHAPTER 5

THE BREAKDOWN
OF THE CREDIT SYSTEM

It appears that we face a problem far worse than a slow, stagnating erosion of profitability in our banks and thrifts. We face the reality that our credit system is holding together only through what is, in effect, a hidden government subsidy—a subsidy that has its limits. You do not need to be prescient to know that whenever we have either a recession, or a rise in short-term rates, or both together, we are going to have some enormous credit problems that will fall, at the end of the day, on the shoulders of the taxpayers. Nor do you have to be prescient to know that when the public understands the full costs of the eventual bailout, the outcry will probably lead to fundamental changes in the laws and structures regulating our financial system.

Going forward, the commercial banking industry will probably have fewer problems than the thrift industry. Right now, regulators appear to be at a loss to help either one. Let me elaborate.

COMMERCIAL BANKING SYSTEM
STILL VIABLE

Thanks to more careful regulation (among other things), the commercial banking industry is still relatively strong. On the other hand, it has plenty of problems. If, as the evidence seems to indicate, there has been a systemic breakdown in credit underwriting standards by a large fraction of the industry over the last several years, we have yet to see how bad the results will be.

Ask anyone who has worked for a bank that has had credit problems. The first large reported loan losses are always just the tip of the iceberg. Once credit problems appear, they usually just keep coming—for several reasons. First, common and bad assumptions have been built into the underwriting of a large part of the portfolio. For example, if the interest rate risk of borrowers has been ignored, all borrowers exposed to interest rate risk are affected should rates rise. Second, unforeseen cross-linkages pull large blocks of business down. For example, the decline of oil prices in the 1980s hurt the Texas economy, which in turn hurt fundamental real estate values just as office space, built in anticipation of a continuing oil boom, came on the market. Thus, loan loss problems that started with independent oil producers migrated to real estate. Third, there is a natural human tendency to cover up bad news. When jobs and careers are at stake, the tendency of most people is to maintain a crossed-fingers, wait-and-see attitude as long as possible. The result is that it takes years to realize the full magnitude of bad credit decisions; in Texas it had taken until 1988 to see just how bad the credit decisions made in 1980 through 1984 actually were.

How bad might the losses be if credit portfolios have already deteriorated because of bad underwriting over the last several years? We cannot predict with certainty, but we can do a simple extrapolation of trends. In Exhibit 5–1, curve 1 shows the distribution of credit losses for the commercial banking industry in 1981. Curve 2 shows the distribution of credit losses for the commercial banking industry in 1986. The existing insurance system will be under severe pressure when a significant number of institutions experience loan losses that are too large to be absorbed out of their own capital. Assuming that it is capitalized to regulatory required levels, a bank that writes off 4 percent of its loans for two years is likely to run out of capital, and losses after that will have to be absorbed by the FDIC, which today has some $20 billion in capital. In 1986 roughly 5 percent of the industry was charging off roughly 4 percent of loans. At that rate, the system was barely hold-

EXHIBIT 5–1
Commercial Bank Net Charge-offs/Loans and Leases, 1981 vs. 1986

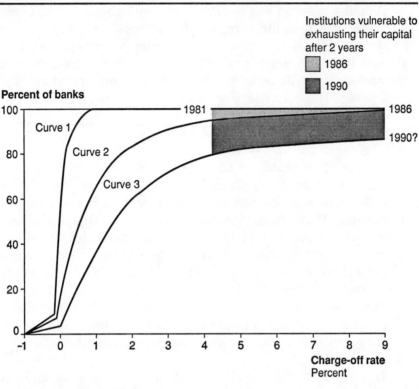

Institutions vulnerable to
exhausting their capital
after 2 years

■ 1986
■ 1990

Percent of banks

Curve 1
Curve 2
Curve 3

1981
1986
1990?

Charge-off rate
Percent

Sources: FDIC; McKinsey analysis

ing its own (i.e., FDIC reserves remained relatively constant).
Curve 3 is a simple extrapolation of that curve into the 1990s,
and it assumes that credit underwriting standards continued
to deteriorate through 1987. If this curve turns out to be true,
roughly 20 percent of the industry's institutions, representing
some $500 billion in assets, will be exhausting their capital
during the early 1990s. If so, the cost of liquidation would be
in the $75 to $100 billion range (i.e., 10 to 15 percent of assets).
In this worst case scenario, the FDIC's reserves would be more
than wiped out.

Even if it proves inappropriate to extrapolate curve 3 (i.e.,
if it turns out that credit underwriting standards have not

deteriorated past 1986 levels), we could still have massive problems should there be a recession. In the period from 1982 to 1986, despite robust growth and falling interest rates, commercial bank charge-offs grew from $6.6 billion to $17 billion. Past experience has shown that in recessions charge-offs usually double or triple. If we were to have a severe recession, and if purely domestic charge-offs were to triple from today's levels, commercial bank charge-offs could reach $50 billion a year. If current patterns hold, roughly one-third of those charge-offs (i.e., $15 to $20 billion) would fall on the weakest 20 percent of the banks in the industry, which has only $16 billion in capital today. In other words, a severe recession could wipe out most of the capital of the weakest banks in the system in a single year. Since high recessionary charge-offs tend to persist for at least two years, the FDIC would have to use its reserves to protect the depositors in the weakest banks. The system would hold—just barely—but the FDIC insurance fund would be depleted. Of course, at this point these are only sobering scenarios. But what was once unthinkable is now a possibility.

THRIFT INDUSTRY IN EXTREMIS

If the future of commercial banks is sobering to contemplate, the future of the thrift industry looks downright grim, even without a recession. Since the tangible net worth of the S&L industry in 1986 was about 1.5 percent of its assets (i.e., $15 billion), there is very little cushion indeed against bad loans. That makes the thrifts far more reliant on government agency insurance, and there is not enough of that in reserve to rationalize the system either.

It is difficult to obtain precise data from the Federal Home Loan Bank Board, but what we have gotten suggests that the cost of liquidating the nation's insolvent thrifts is already staggering, even if we manage to avoid a recession or a further increase in interest rates.

As a point of comparison, the cost to the FDIC of liquidating a commercial bank is about 10 to 15 percent of that bank's assets. Failed thrifts, on the other hand, cost the FSLIC much more to liquidate, because the typical insolvent thrift has much less value of its own. Not only does it begin with a reported negative net worth, but even that worth is overstated, since many of its assets are nonperforming loans that are obviously worth less than their face value, and many others are mortgages and securities that have a market value well below the value shown on the balance sheet. In the last few months of 1987 and in early 1988, thrifts liquidated by the FSLIC had a cost of over 30 percent of assets.

At that rate, since the GAAP insolvent thrifts have about $135 billion in assets, the cost of liquidating this group would be between $40 billion and $50 billion. Moreover, many of the low net worth thrifts may also actually be insolvent. Since these thrifts hold another $250 billion in assets, the cost of liquidating this second group could be an additional $40 billion, assuming a lesser 15 percent liquidation cost. The FSLIC has no intention of liquidating this group, since their focus is on the already insolvent institutions. In the event of a recession or a major run-up of interest rates, however, this second group would also become massively insolvent. If so, the cost of bailing out both these sets of institutions, with assets of some $400 billion, could easily exceed $100 billion.

Thrift industry defenders label such estimates as "absurd" and place the "real" numbers closer to $25 to $40 billion. But the truth is that it is impossible to estimate accurately how much cash will be needed, because no one knows the "real" value of the assets now on the books of weak thrifts, or whether we will have a recession, or a run-up in interest rates. Only time will tell.

Against this problem, at the end of 1987 the FSLIC had a negative net worth and permission to recapitalize itself to the tune of $10.8 billion (through new public bond issues that are to be raised through providing the bondholders with a first claim on incoming deposit insurance premiums). Clearly, this sum is grossly inadequate to permit the liquidation of all the insolvent thrifts. Keeping insolvent thrifts open is very dangerous, since they will lose more money while they continue to operate, making the ultimate losses upon liquidation even greater.

REGULATORY ACTION INADEQUATE

The Federal Home Loan Bank Board and the FSLIC, after passing through a period in the mid-1980s that can only be characterized as benign neglect, are now doing the best they can to contain the problems in the industry. New regulators are in place, but they are, frankly, overwhelmed by the magnitude of the task that faces them relative to their staff size and relative to the cash available to them to address the cash problems they face.

For example, the FSLIC used some of the cash from its new borrowing authority to restructure the Vernon Savings and Loan of Dallas, Texas. This institution had some 80 percent of its loans on nonaccrual. Best estimates are that if the FSLIC had liquidated this thrift and paid off depositors, it might have cost 70 to 80 percent of the agency's assets to liquidate this institution (i.e., $800 to $900 million)—as well as opening up the FSLIC to potential legal liabilities of an additional $2 billion. Instead, the FSLIC took over Vernon's nearly worthless assets and substituted a note from itself for $1.1 billion plus $200 million in cash. In other words, the FSLIC in effect must pay interest on about $1 billion in debt, in perpetuity, so it can continue paying interest to Vernon's depositors. That is, the FSLIC is committed to paying roughly $100 million a year, for the foreseeable future, just to keep $1.3 billion of deposits current. Obviously, Vernon is an extreme example. But the annual carrying costs of using such an approach for any significant fraction of the $135 billion of deposits of GAAP insolvent thrifts would be prohibitive.

Indeed, while precise numbers are not available, our best estimate is that it is already taking some $7 to $10 billion per year of new cash to keep the existing system from collapsing on itself, excluding any of the money needed for direct cash infusions from the FSLIC. This is cash in the form of deposits raised under government guarantees to cover the cash drain of operating losses (as in the Ponzi scheme outlined earlier). In addition, some cash is provided directly by the FSLIC to directly subsidize failing thrifts—perhaps another $5 to $8 billion a year is now being supplied. Thus, the government is, in effect, now subsidizing the operations of insolvent thrifts at a rate of $12 to $15 billion a year, or more, with no end in sight. The good news is that such a subsidy is still a small number in comparison to the $1 trillion annual federal budget. The bad news is that because the underlying problem is systemic, it will get worse and worse until the regulatory structure of the industry is changed.

Commercial bankers may wonder what concern it is of theirs that the weakest members of the thrift industry are being massively subsidized by the federal government. It should be of great concern, for a few reasons. First, it seems likely that the weakest commercial banks will soon follow the weakest thrifts in also having massive insolvency problems. Second, like it or not, the fate of the FDIC and indeed of all depository insurance will be tied to the fate of the FSLIC when the costs of the subsidy become apparent to taxpayers. Finally, it seems reasonable to expect that depository institution regulation will be rewritten for both industries simultaneously.

The bank regulators certainly share concerns about the nation's credit problems. The U.S. commercial bank regulators, the Federal Reserve, the FDIC, and the Comptroller of the Currency are doing everything that they can *with their existing policy tools* to protect the system. They are vigorously auditing commercial banks, stopping unsound lending practices where they find them, forcing the restructuring of banks where that option has the lowest cost to the federal deposit insurance fund, and so forth. Indeed, by most measures they are doing a remarkably effective job in making the traditional system work as best it can under very difficult circumstances.

They are also trying to improve the regulatory framework. Our bank regulators, in concert with their counterparts in other countries, have proposed a set of capital adequacy guidelines aimed at raising the worldwide level of required bank capital by 1992 and adjusting those guidelines for risk. The objective is to move toward common standards worldwide and a safer global credit system. In fact, this proposal is the single most important regulatory response to the breakdown of the credit system.

Unfortunately, the proposed revisions have most of the same flaws that our current regulations have. First, they do not define sources for new capital. In the United States, where will banks that need capital find it? Without satisfactory earnings banks can neither grow the capital they need through retained earnings nor issue new stock.

A second, and more important, flaw is that the proposed guidelines make no provision for matching capital requirements to differences in loan quality; remember, this has been the downfall of our struggling banks so far. Under the proposal (as under the current system) all loans are to have the same capital requirements, whether the borrower is a triple-A company or a potential bankrupt. If the proposal becomes law, banks will still earn such low spreads on high-quality, floating-rate debt that they will be unable to justify the capital needed to book the business. Instead, because the capital requirements for both high- and low-risk loans will be the same, banks will continue to be motivated to book high credit-risk loans (e.g., acquisition debt, leveraged-buyout finance) or high interest-rate-risk loans (e.g., fixed-rate mortgages). Only these will yield spreads high enough to generate a satisfactory return on equity.

A third fatal flaw of the proposed guidelines is that they, like the existing regulations, implicitly assume that all banks are the same. This assumption is clearly invalid; in fact, the evidence is that competition is causing banks to become more divergent. The weakest banks (and thrifts) obviously need far more capital to protect the depository insurance funds from loss, but the strongest banks are overcapitalized even now relative to the risks they are taking.

When we match concentrated charge-offs against capital, we see that commercial banking industry-wide regulatory capital requirements are beside the point (Exhibit 5–2). In 1986 the strongest 70 percent of the industry had $173 billion in primary capital, but charge-offs of only $8 billion. That is, their capital was 21 times greater than their charge-offs. In contrast, the weakest 10 percent of the industry had $7.6 billion in primary capital and charge-offs of $3.5 billion. You cannot charge off at the rate of half your capital a year for very long and stay in business—at least in most businesses.

When asked about the illogic of requiring uniform capital guidelines for highly differentiated categories of loans, or

EXHIBIT 5–2
Commercial Banks Ranked by Net Charge-offs/Loans and Leases, 1986

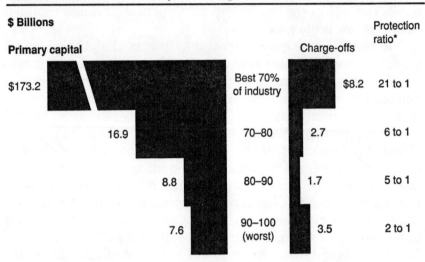

$ Billions				Protection ratio*
Primary capital			Charge-offs	
$173.2		Best 70% of industry	$8.2	21 to 1
	16.9	70–80	2.7	6 to 1
	8.8	80–90	1.7	5 to 1
	7.6	90–100 (worst)	3.5	2 to 1

*Primary capital/charge-offs.

Sources: FDIC; McKinsey analysis

for institutions with highly differentiated exposures to risks, regulators reply that a more differentiated system would "be unworkably complex." And they are right. The problem is analogous to price controls; price controls and competition are incompatible. In a capitalist economy price controls always break down. They become too complex to administer, and they force supply and demand imbalances, which adjust through evasion in the black markets. The problem with combining capital guidelines and competition is similar; high-quality credit risk (for which the capital guidelines are too high) will bypass the industry while low-quality credit (for which the capital guidelines are too low) will be attracted to the industry.

The truth is capital adequacy guidelines are a blind alley unless other changes are made in the structure.

Something must be done, but it must be something new. We cannot return to the same kind of controls we had in the postwar era. The government could not reimpose deposit interest ceilings today. The political power of depositors (e.g., the nation's retirees) is enormous, and they are too sophisticated financially to allow themselves to be taken advantage of again. Similarly, borrowers have learned how to play institutions off against one another. As long as there is more lending capacity than demand for loans, borrowers will be able to pick and choose among a great many banks, thrifts, and even nonbanks (e.g., General Electric Credit Corporation, General Motors Acceptance Corporation). Once competition has been introduced, there is no going back. The genie is out of the bottle.

An air of unreality continues to pervade discussion of the breakdown of the credit system with regulators, bankers, legislators, and other informed participants. Most of the focus is on LDC debt rather than the breakdown of the system as a whole. No one disputes the basic facts, but no one wants to act on them either—because no one sees what he or she personally can do about the situation and because the facts are unpleasant. Everyone simply wants the problem to go away.

But it will not. The basic dynamics of the credit system are unsound. Left alone, weak banks and thrifts will continue to make bad loans—more and more of them. Hopelessly insolvent institutions will not be miraculously cured.

At some point over the next several years, if current trends continue, we are likely to face a watershed crisis that will provoke massive changes in our financial and regulatory system. The precipitating event may be the FSLIC's admission that it lacks the cash needed by insolvent thrifts and the resulting flight of uninsured depositors from these institutions. Or it may be the insolvency and failure of one or more of the LDC money center banks weakened by write-offs (some of these would have almost no equity capital at all if their LDC debt was marked to market). Or it may be a rise in short-term interest rates that causes the flow of red ink in many commercial banks and thrifts to be so heavy as to scare all uninsured depositors. Or it may be a recession that causes credit losses so massive that the FDIC joins the FSLIC as an insolvent insurance fund.

The evidence is building daily that the credit system is going to break down sooner than I expected it to when I started writing this book. As I am doing my final edit, I read that the First City Bancorporation (Houston) bailout is being threatened by bond arbitrageurs, that the FDIC is issuing a blanket guarantee of all First Republic Bancorporation's banking subsidiaries' deposits (plus committing as much as $4.5 billion in funds), and that the FSLIC is also issuing a blanket guarantee of the Financial Corporation of America's main thrift unit. Just these three institutions account for $70 billion in assets. I also read that one-third of the nation's thrifts lost money in 1987— a group total loss of over $13 billion. Some 500 S&Ls are now insolvent using Generally Accepted Accounting Principles. The situation is deteriorating rapidly.

Whenever the precipitating event takes place, massive government intervention will be required to maintain confidence in depository institutions. Such intervention will probably include billions of dollars of direct cash from taxpayers. When this occurs, public outrage will ensure that the existing system is changed.

There are some encouraging signs that the legislative gridlock in Washington is beginning to break up. As of this writing, legislation that would largely abolish the obsolete Glass-Steagall barriers between the banking and securities industries is winding its way through Congress. But there seems to be little will in the Congress to take on the core issue: the breakdown of the credit system. Indeed, it will probably take public outrage to convince the Congress to address that one.

The outcome of that process, whenever it happens, is hard to predict. We might end up with new legislation and regulation that makes a bad situation worse. We might have a "witch hunt," leading to overly restrictive regulation that completes the destruction of the commercial banking and thrift industries—including the good institutions as well as the bad. That would be tragedy for the nation as well as the institutions.

However, we might also wind up with a better, more effective system—a system designed for competition. In the next part of this book I will propose one such system; there are other models being proposed by others as well. We need to weigh their relative merits now, so that we are prepared whenever the precipitating event occurs. The model proposed in this book is based upon the widespread adoption of a new technology for lending: structured securitized credit. Using this technology, it is possible to rethink the models for both how a bank operates and how a bank is regulated.

PART 2

RETHINKING
THE BANK

CHAPTER 6

STRUCTURED SECURITIZED CREDIT: A SUPERIOR TECHNOLOGY FOR LENDING

Structured securitized credit is a new technology for lending that has been developed essentially by nonbankers. It is better on all counts than the traditional lending system. It is growing very rapidly precisely because it is a superior technology—one that, in fact, is rendering traditional banking obsolete. Many bankers see this as a problem; I see it as part of a solution. At a time when the traditional lending system is clearly in trouble, this new technology is offering us a framework for a fundamentally different and better financial system.

Just as the electronics industry was transformed when vacuum tubes were replaced by transistors, and transistors were then replaced by integrated circuits, the financial services industry is being transformed now that securitized credit is beginning to replace traditional lending. Like other technological transformations, this one will take place over years, not overnight. We estimate it will take 10 to 15 years for structured securitized credit to displace completely the classic banking system—not a long time, considering that the fundamentals of banking have remained essentially unchanged since the Middle Ages.

When the electronics industry was transformed, some players who could not adapt to the new technology lost out—although the public was, in general, better off. In this financial transformation, however, the casualties could reach further. Banks and thrifts depend on the old technology, and these institutions underpin our national economy; if they are threatened, we are all exposed. Left to its own, the new technology could accelerate their destruction. Properly managed, however, it could also save the banking industry—preserving the value of its existing franchise by enabling banks to serve their customers without cross-subsidy.

The longer we at McKinsey have thought about it, the more convinced we have become that structured securitized credit is a superior technology. We feared it at first because of its potential to take good assets off the balance sheets of banks, which already face a shortage of high-quality assets. But the more we have examined the issues, the more we have understood that it is the traditional depository system, regulated by the current laws and structures, that is the fundamental problem. In fact, far from threatening the well-being of well-managed commercial banks and thrifts, this new technology could enable them to prosper.

Before describing how this could work, I would like to describe the new technology in some detail. When you understand how it works, you will more easily see how it could form the basis for a new banking system.

WHAT IS STRUCTURED SECURITIZED CREDIT?

Structured securitized credit is a hybrid form of financing that combines features of two well-developed systems: the traditional credit system and the securities system. Since there is considerable confusion over terms, even among participants in the technology, I will begin with some definitions. When I say *securitization*, I mean the trend toward financial assets being securities rather than loans. When I say *structured securitized credit*, I mean the form of securitization in which loans are literally converted into securities. Securitization can take place without credit securitization. For example, commercial paper issuance is a form of securitization that does not involve the literal conversion of loans into securities. Most of this chapter will be about credit securitization. But that new technology is easier to understand if you remember its origins.

Since its beginnings in medieval Europe, as described in Chapter 1, bank lending has been a relatively straightforward business. Ever since money changers and goldsmiths began accepting funds for safekeeping and lending out the idle cash to credit-worthy borrowers, the fundamentals of banking have remained the same. Banks have provided depositors with safe, liquid instruments in which to invest their funds and have taken those funds and lent them to borrowers. In the process, banks have absorbed the credit risk inherent in any lending process. Safety to depositors has been provided by the bank's capital or, more recently, by government backing in the form of deposit insurance or other support. Other lenders, like consumer and commercial finance companies, have employed the same basic business system—except that they have raised funds by either issuing securities or borrowing from banks instead of accepting deposits. One of the chief advantages of the traditional credit system is that close personal relationships often develop between the borrower and the lender; these relationships are particularly important for small borrowers. Indeed, it is in these relationships that banks add the most value to their customers. Going forward, it is these relationships that need to be retained in any new banking system.

The securities system, of course, was separated from the commercial banking system in this country in the 1930s. Debt securities differ from loans made by banks in that the debt is *issued*—that is, the debt instruments are sold to the public at large and then traded among investors until they are redeemed by the issuer according to the terms of the original issue. Over the last decade much of the borrowing that traditionally flowed through the credit system has been migrating to the securities system. This is because, as we saw in Chapter 2, securities are inherently a more efficient, more cost-effective method of borrowing.

Where does that cost effectiveness come from? For most securities it comes from the two big advantages that securities offer to the source of funds: the end investors. First, securities are liquid and tradable, while loans are illiquid; there is only a very limited secondary market for most loans. Partly, this liquidity stems from the fact that the value of a debt security is determined by the market. In contrast, the value of a loan is based upon subjective valuation. What is the real value of a loan made to Mexico? Book value? Fifty percent of book? Seventy percent of book?

The second advantage of debt securities is that they are rated by credit agencies, while loans are not. Large classes of investors have little ability or desire to assess or cope with credit risk (these include individuals and pension funds). By investing in rated securities, these groups avoid the trouble and expense of dealing with credit risk, assessing credit worthiness, or working out problem loans to avoid large losses.

Historically, investors have been willing to pay for the greater liquidity and credit transparency of securities over loans by accepting lower returns than the equivalent loan would provide. This, in turn, has led borrowers who raise money through securities to have lower financing costs, provided the costs of issuing the securities do not exceed the differential between the interest rate on the security and its loan equivalent. Today, this generally means they need to borrow at least $100 million at a time, since issues below that size are too illiquid to appeal to investors and the costs of issuing are too great relative to the cost savings. As a result, the securities markets have traditionally been open only to large, high-quality borrowers such as the U.S. Treasury or investment grade corporations. Where there has been a choice, most borrowers have opted for securities. Few large, high-quality corporations have borrowed money from commercial banks in recent years. At the same time, as described earlier in the book, the outstanding nonbank commercial paper issued in the United States has grown from $40 billion to over $300 billion since 1975.

Banks have retained the business of other borrowers, including all individuals and all mid-sized and smaller corporations, largely by default. No matter how credit worthy, these borrowers have been excluded from issuing debt securities and enjoying their advantages.

But this is now changing. Investment bankers, led by Drexel Burnham, have been working hard in recent years to extend the benefits of securitization to borrowers that do not meet the traditional criteria, and in the process these bankers have changed the risk profile of securities. For example, new issues of junk bonds grew from $3 billion a year in 1982 to $34 billion a year in 1986. These debt securities have the credit risk of loans.

Responding to this trend, some traditional lenders have begun to treat some of their loans like securities. The excess capacity created by the large number of banks and investors willing to lend to large, high-grade corporations has created razor-thin spreads, under .25 percent. These low spreads, in combination with the increasing capital requirements from U.S. regulators mentioned earlier, have made it impossible for U.S. commercial banks to lend money to high-grade corporations and earn reasonable returns on their shareholders' capital. As a result, banks have been looking for ways to satisfy their borrowers' credit needs without putting loans on their balance sheets. For example, many major U.S. banks have sold loans outright to other institutions. Loan sales in just the United States grew from almost nonexistent outstandings in 1982 to about $35 billion by the end of 1986.

Many people associate the term *loan sales* or *asset sales* with credit securitization, and much publicity has been attached to these activities. However, the volume of loans that can be sold without recourse is very limited, since the only loans that can be sold in this manner are large loans to relatively high-grade companies, whose credit worthiness the purchaser has already analyzed. We estimate that only roughly $50 billion of such loans still remain on bank balance sheets (out of some $2.7 trillion in assets). Moreover, such loan sales add very little value, since there is no restructuring of the credit being extended. As a result, spreads on these loan sales are microscopic; the total profit for the selling bank may only be 10 basis points or less. Finally, some observers are very worried about the documentation of these sold loans. In some cases, it is unclear whether the selling bank has accomplished a "true sale."

Overall, securitization through all of these forms (commercial paper, bonds, junk bonds, and loan sales) has been expanding very rapidly. However, many of these forms appear to be approaching their limits of growth.

Most of the remaining $4.4 trillion of loans on the balance sheets of all U.S. depository institutions, finance companies, and corporations (even corporations make loans, largely through trade receivables) cannot be securitized using any of these old techniques. Most of the borrowers involved are either mid-sized or smaller corporations or individuals. Before these assets can be removed from their respective balance sheets, they must literally be converted into securities using the *structured securitized credit technology*.

HOW STRUCTURED SECURITIZED CREDIT WORKS

At the heart of the new technology is the *structuring* process. Before they can be converted into securities, most loans must be structured to transform the quality of risk and returns to the end investors. Structuring includes the explicit underwriting and absorption of credit risk, usually through credit enhancement, and the use of special purpose vehicles. Because the term *structured securitized credit* is cumbersome, I will shorten it to *securitized credit* from now on.

Securitized credit combines elements of traditional lending with elements of traditional securities, but it also involves processes and structures not conceived of in either traditional system. Under the traditional lending system, the same institution (a commercial bank, a thrift, or a finance company) would originate the loan, structure the terms, absorb the credit risk, fund the asset, and service the collection of principal payments and interest. Under the new system, several different institutions might be involved, each playing a different functional role. For example, in extending credit under the new system, one institution could originate the loan, a second institution (probably an investment bank) could structure the transaction into a security, a third institution could insure the credit risk, a fourth institution could place the security with an investor and trade the security in the secondary market, and, finally, a fifth institution could service the underlying loans (Exhibit 6–1).

EXHIBIT 6–1
Credit Securitization Changing Traditional Commercial Banking Business System

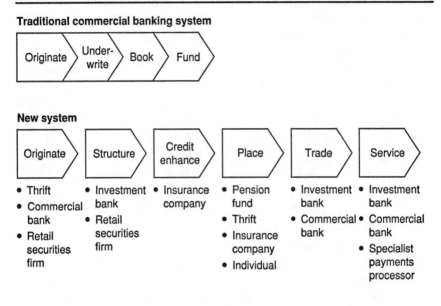

Traditional commercial banking system

Originate > Under-write > Book > Fund

New system

Originate > Structure > Credit enhance > Place > Trade > Service

- Thrift
- Commercial bank
- Retail securities firm

- Investment bank
- Retail securities firm

- Insurance company

- Pension fund
- Thrift
- Insurance company
- Individual

- Investment bank
- Commercial bank

- Investment bank
- Commercial bank
- Specialist payments processor

Securitized credit is an outgrowth of a U.S. government-backed mortgage pass-through program started in the mid-1970s, whereby residential mortgages were first pooled together, then guaranteed by the U.S. government, and then sold as securities to end investors by securities firms.

The driving force behind this new technology over the last several years has been the U.S. investment banking industry (particularly First Boston, Salomon Brothers, and more recently such players as Merrill Lynch and Goldman Sachs). Investment banks developed the process for securitizing government-guaranteed mortgages and then used it to securitize privately issued residential mortgages, commercial mortgages, automobile loans, credit card receivables, and even commercial loans and lease receivables (work is being done now on other classes of assets). Obviously, the incentives for the investment banks are substantial underwriting fees and trading profits, which can be gained in markets that were formerly controlled by banks and thrifts (i.e., the borrowings of individuals, mid-sized companies, small businesses, and private companies).

There are four financial innovations that investment bankers have used to convert loans into securities and to make the resulting securities more valuable.

1. *Special purpose vehicles.* A special purpose vehicle is a trust or corporation that has been established for the sole purpose of owning the loans. The special purpose vehicle then issues securities, which are bought by investors. Its exact form depends on: the specific nature and risks of the assets; relevant legal, regulatory, and tax issues; and the objectives of the funds raiser. In every case, however, its purpose is to isolate the risks inherent in the loans placed in it from all the other risks of the funds raiser.

2. *Pooling of borrowers.* Through the special purpose vehicle, loans to different borrowers are pooled together in order to reach the minimum size (roughly $100 million) necessary to justify a public securities issue. In addition, this pooling diversifies the credit risk.

3. *Credit structuring and enhancement.* When a pool of loans and the collateral for the loans are segregated in a special purpose vehicle, a credit underwriter (a commercial bank, finance company, or insurance company) can assess and underwrite the credit risk in that specific pool of loans and then guarantee the credit risk. Such a guarantee can raise the credit risk of the pool to investment grade levels. This in turn allows individuals, pension funds, and other classes of investors who have neither the skill nor the desire to assess credit risk to invest in the securities issued by the special purpose vehicle. In some cases, the careful structuring of the transaction is sufficient to allow the issue to be rated by a rating agency. In that case no additional credit guarantee is required.

4. *Repackaging of cash flows.* In some cases the special purpose vehicle has repackaged the cash flows from the loans. For example, a collateralized mortgage obligation (CMO) is a special purpose vehicle structure that has been used to purchase mortgage loans and then issue tranches of varying maturity (e.g., a fast-pay, a medium-pay, and a slow-pay tranche) backed by the underlying loans. Each of these tranches has a different expected life that reflects the expected prepayment patterns of the underlying mortgages. As the loans are paid off by borrowers, the principal first goes to the first tranche until it is paid off, then to the second tranche, and so forth.

This structure enables the packager, which is usually an investment bank, to tailor the cash flows of the different tranches to appeal to particular investor preferences. In a CMO a thrift might purchase a shorter tranche, while a longer-term investor like a pension fund might purchase a longer tranche. This repackaging of cash flows also allows the packagers to create tranches with different prepayment risk characteristics.

To see how these financial innovations make the securitization of credit possible, let's look at three examples.

In September 1985, Franklin Savings sold $100 million in U.S. government-guaranteed loans to a special purpose trust, which issued eight-year bonds. The bonds were overcollateralized. Salomon underwrote the issue. In this case, the credit structuring (i.e., overcollateralization of the bonds) enabled the issue to be rated AAA. This transaction was very similar to many other mortgage-backed bonds issued by other thrifts.

In December 1985, Olympia & York (a large owner of commercial real estate properties) placed a mortgage on its building located at 59 Maiden Lane in New York City. Olympia & York created a special purpose trust, which issued 10-year notes for $200 million. This issue provided for annual interest payments and stipulated that the principal would be paid back entirely, in a single payment, by no later than the end of the tenth year. The mortgage and lease payments were used as collateral. Ninety percent of the space was leased by two high quality tenants (one of which represented quasi-government risk) whose leases expired after the maturity of the notes. Aetna Insurance guaranteed $30 million in interest payments to investors. The combination of the structuring of the credit and the guarantee enabled the issue to be rated AAA. The issue was lead managed by Salomon Brothers International.

In October 1986, the automobile financing arm for General Motors (GMAC) initiated the largest financial transaction ever completed by a single private issuer. This was a $4 billion new issue, backed by low-interest rate (under 5 percent) vehicle loans that had been used by GMAC to promote the sale of new automobiles. First Boston packaged and was the lead underwriter for the deal. First Boston created a special purpose vehicle called the Asset-Backed Securities Corporation (ABSC) to purchase the automobile loans from GMAC and to issue notes to investors. The notes were issued in a fast-pay, a medium-pay, and a slow-pay tranche. Investors were protected from the credit risk in several ways. First, GMAC provided a first loss limited guarantee of 5 percent. This was far in excess of GMAC's expected loss history on similar loans, which was under 1 percent. In addition, First Boston had invested $40 million in capital in ABSC, which provided an additional 1 percent protection. Finally, Credit Suisse (a AAA bank with a higher credit rating than GMAC's AA+) backed up the 6 percent first loss credit guarantee by GMAC and ABSC by issuing a standby letter of credit that insured the timely payment of principal and interest. This combination of credit enhancements enabled the security to be rated AAA by Standard and Poor's (Exhibit 6–2).

As you can see, these transactions can become mind-numbingly complex. These three examples were selected from the several hundreds of structured securitized credit transactions that have been done in the last few years. The specific terms of each transaction tend to be very precisely defined and different from other transactions, because much of the value added by securitized credit is in the very precise tailoring of terms to the very specific characteristics of the assets and the particular needs of investors. It is, therefore, very hard to describe a typical deal.

Because of their complexity, these transactions depend heavily on another kind of technology: computers. Computer systems have played a vital role in two ways.

1. *Funds tracking.* These kinds of transactions would not even be possible without computers to, first, keep track of cash flows and loan defaults from individual loans and, second, ensure that all participants get exactly the returns due them. To make this process work, each loan and interest payment must be tagged as it flows from the borrower, to the intermediary who made the loan, to the special purpose vehicle, and, finally, to the end investor who bought the security. Moreover,

EXHIBIT 6-2
Asset-Backed Securities Corporation, October 1986

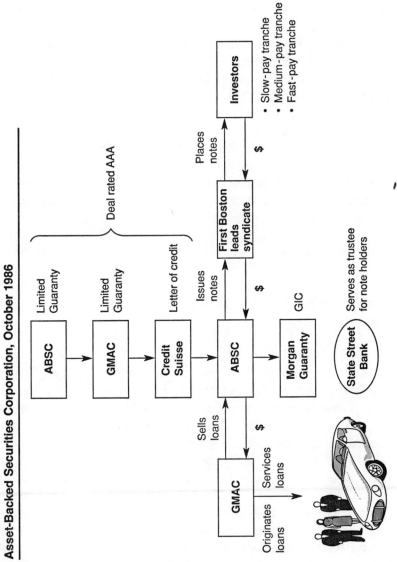

all of these transfers must be documented in accordance with complex legal requirements to ensure that with each cash payment there is a proper transfer of both return and risk. Without sophisticated computers, all of this would be impossible.

2. *Analysis*. Computer-based analysis of cash flows is critical to understanding the expected returns for all participants, and it is particularly important for understanding the credit risk and the prepayment risk inherent in the transactions. For example, some of the leading investment banks involved in this business have spent enormous energy analyzing the prepayment risks of different kinds of residential mortgages. Some of them, indeed, have analyzed the demographics of mortgage prepayments even down to prepayment patterns by postal zip code. These analyses enable them to build the complex tranche structures that are often critical to these types of transactions.

HOW FAST SECURITIZED CREDIT HAS GROWN

As mentioned earlier, the securitized credit technology has already been applied to government-insured mortgages, privately insured mortgages, automobile loans, credit card receivables, commercial mortgages, and even commercial loan receivables. The oldest form of securitized credit, mortgage-backed securities, has grown tremendously since its introduction in the mid-1970s. By the end of 1986 about $600 billion in mortgage-backed securities was outstanding, and we estimate that this volume grew by 25 to 30 percent during 1987 to a total of approximately $750 billion. This $750 billion figure actually exceeds the total loans made by all commercial banks to all the nation's businesses; as of June 1987 the entire commercial banking system had a total of about $500 billion in commercial and industrial loans outstanding. Mortgage-backed securities were originally issued only by government-related entities; now, however, private issuers are becoming increasingly important. During 1987 new mortgage-backed securities issues (both public and private) represented about two-thirds of all mortgage originations in that year. There were over 360 privately sponsored new issues in 1987, or 1.5 every business day, for an annual volume of $70 billion.

The securitization of nonmortgage loans through special purpose vehicles has only begun to take place, but it looks like volume is going to grow equally rapidly. Car loans, which were first securitized in 1984, grew from new issues totaling only $140 million in that year, to $1 billion in 1985, to $8.5 billion in 1986 (excluding several significantly sized private placements of structured securitized loans). In 1987, a number of new issuers appeared: GMAC was joined by General Electric Credit Corporation, Marine Midland, Chrysler Financial, and Mack (Truck) Financial. The roster of underwriters has also lengthened; First Boston and Salomon Brothers have been joined by several investment banks (Goldman Sachs, Drexel Burnham, Shearson Lehman, and Kidder, Peabody), as well as a commercial bank (Marine Midland).

Credit card receivables were securitized for essentially the first time in 1986 ($850 million). It appears that the volume of these kinds of receivables had more than tripled by the end of 1987. And the end is nowhere in sight. Many players are now working hard to develop structures for securitizing non-standardized residential mortgages, commercial and industrial loans, lease receivables, and commercial assets. What is particularly significant is that this technology is winning against a subsidized system. Remember, banks today are lending at rates that reflect federally guaranteed deposits and other safety nets. If these were removed and lending rates rose to market-driven levels, the advantage of securitized credit would be even greater.

Despite all the growth, only about 35 percent of home mortgages, 5 percent of auto loans, 1 percent of commercial mortgages, and 2 percent of credit card loans in the United States had been securitized by the end of 1987 (Exhibit 6–3). All told, securitized loans represented $770 billion of outstandings by the end of 1987—compared to the total of over $4 trillion of potentially securitizable assets (Exhibit 6–4). I expect securitized credit to continue to make large inroads into loans in the years ahead, although a number of factors are slowing it down.

Some of these factors are the common growing pains of

EXHIBIT 6–3
Amount of Credit Securitized, 1987 ($Billions Outstanding)

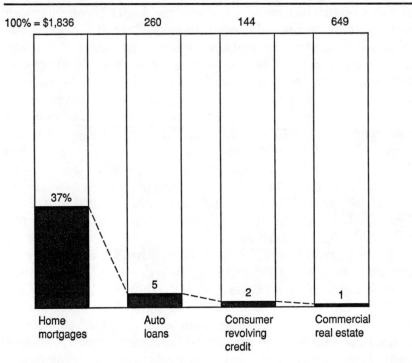

Sources: Federal Reserve; McKinsey estimates

any financial service business: few people and much to learn. While there are now large numbers of investment bankers and traders with the skills to structure and make markets in the new instruments, there is a shortage of people in the originating institutions who have sufficient skill to work with them. It will take years before there are sufficient numbers of skilled individuals available.

And even the people with the best skills are still, by and large, feeling their way. As a result, it can take from six months to over a year of detailed work by originators with lawyers, accountants, and investment bankers to bring a new, very sophisticated, very complex financing to the point where it can be underwritten and placed. Much of this time is devoted to determining how the credit risk is to be structured and

EXHIBIT 6–4
Securitizable Asset Classes, 1986 ($Trillions Outstanding)

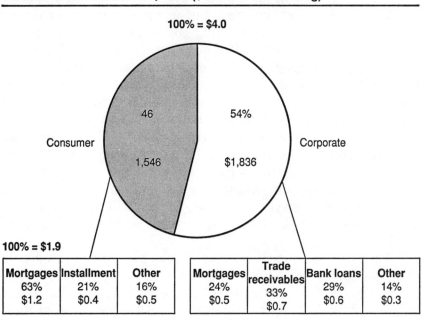

Source: McKinsey analysis

absorbed. Given the newness of the instruments, neither regulators, nor rating agencies, nor potential guarantors are exactly sure what rules should be followed. There is some learning curve in effect, but every time an institution wants to issue a new instrument, it must invest many person-years of effort in working out documentation and servicing procedures before it can begin to offer a new instrument to its customers.

Some of these deals involve not only a big investment in development, but also high administrative costs. When loans are not originated with credit securitization in mind, these costs can be prohibitive. For example, it is very expensive at present to transfer the title on automobile lease receivables. Because these deals still involve so much expense, time, and ambiguity, many potentially securitizable transactions are still being done conventionally. Often, the need to obtain financing is too great to await the resolution of all the uncertainties.

The third factor that is holding back securitized credit, which I will discuss at some length later, is regulation and legal constraints. Perhaps the most important constraint is Glass-Steagall, the U.S. law separating commercial and investment banking. Glass-Steagall restrictions limit the ability of commercial banks to underwrite and make markets in most of these types of securities. As a result, many banks are (with reluctance) forced simply to hand over the business to a Salomon or a First Boston. As this book is being written, legislation has been proposed that would remove Glass-Steagall barriers, but others remain. For example, regulators have forbidden commercial banks from securitizing their own assets using the approach GMAC has used to guarantee its automobile loans (recourse for the 5 percent first loss). This, again, will obviously slow down commercial bank participation in securitizing many of their own loans.

The fourth factor holding back securitized credit is psychological. Most lenders are barely aware of the technology, and many that are aware of it are afraid of it. This is not surprising; in fact, it is characteristic of the response of most entrenched participants in any industry that is confronted with a new technology. In this case, the fear is unfounded. As I will describe later in the chapter, the issuing intermediary reaps substantial benefits from securitizing loans.

These inhibiting factors are common whenever technology changes. It takes time for any new technology, no matter how superior, to replace an established one—partly because it takes time to adapt old methods of operating to the new technology, and partly because it takes time to build the infrastructure of support needed for the technology.

For example, when cars were introduced around the turn of the century, manufacturing was very crude. Thousands of small workshops (i.e., job shops) were producing these first vehicles. Moreover, the infrastructure supporting the car was almost nonexistent. Roads were little more than cow paths. There were no service stations, garage mechanics, traffic police, or speed limits. The full impact of the automobile was not felt until the techniques of mass production were adopted and the infrastructure of support for the technology was built. These together lowered the costs and increased the benefits of the car until it was appealing to the mass market.

Securitized credit is still at an early stage in its evolution. The techniques of production are still crude. The infrastructure to support it has not yet been built. It will take time for the new technology to take over. But I would guess that within the next 10 to 15 years, 60 to 80 percent or more of all new loans might well be transformed into securities. The benefits that current players are enjoying and the sheer superiority of the technology over traditional lending are powerful forces for change.

BENEFITS TO CURRENT PLAYERS

I have said that securitized credit is a more efficient, effective technology. It is growing rapidly despite the constraints I have just enumerated, because it offers great benefits to each participant. Let me be more specific.

Benefits to Investors

Why do investors like securitized credit? Chiefly, because securitized credit increases the volume and variety of instruments in which they can invest. For example, some issues have been specifically designed to fit the needs of money market mutual funds. Because there is a shortage of AAA, one-year paper, some issues have been tailored to provide investors with yields of 20 basis points more than they could earn on comparable, highly liquid investments. Given the intensity of the competition among investors for performance, which is one key to their ability to attract new funds, even modest yield increases attract substantial new investment.

Of course, the rates paid by issuers to investors is much lower than the effective yield on the underlying loans (e.g., credit card loans yielding 18 percent are sold with a pass-through yield of 8 to 9 percent). Many observers wonder why this happens; they believe the investor should receive the full spread. But the truth is that investors cannot originate these loans and would not want them in their original form even if they could. They are happy to give up a substantial portion of the loan spread in return for the greater liquidity, credit transparency, and credit risk absorption of securitized loans. The yield requirements of investors are driven by their alternatives for equivalent investments. Thus, on securitized car loans investors have been willing to accept yields of 5 or 6 percent less than the rates paid by the underlying borrowers. For mortgage-backed securities investors are accepting approximately 1 to 1.5 percent less than the rates paid by the underlying borrowers.

Benefits to Issuing Institutions

But who earns the difference in spread between the lower rate the investors are willing to receive for high-quality, liquid paper and the rate borrowers pay?

In the transactions done to date the lion's share of the spread has been retained by the intermediary that made the original loan; this spread is only reduced by the costs of securitizing the loan (i.e., the issuing costs). For example, when credit cards are securitized the intermediary originating the credit card loans retains almost all of the spread between the 18 percent being paid by borrowers and the 7 to 8 percent paid to investors on the securitized paper.

Obviously, it should take only a simple analysis to determine whether or not to securitize a particular class of loans. An intermediary should securitize loans whenever the spread on the securitized loan (net of issuing costs) is greater than the spread earned (net of funding costs) from keeping the loan on the intermediary's balance sheet.

For intermediaries who themselves are not at least single-A credits, it will always pay to securitize high-quality assets, because in doing so they can fund themselves more cheaply. For example, banks that are part holding companies, rated single-A or less, have saved about 1.5 percent in direct financing cost through securitizing loans (e.g. credit card) relative to issuing notes of their own with an equivalent maturity. In other words, for any intermediary of less than single-A quality, the costs of securitizing any assets whose credit quality is higher than its own credit risk will be more than offset by savings in funding costs.

But we can go further than that. Securitizing high-quality assets makes sense for almost any intermediary, even institutions of AAA quality, when one considers the full costs of balance sheet intermediation. For a commercial bank these include the costs of its required reserves, its FDIC insurance, and its regulatory capital requirements. In fact, high-quality lenders would reap their greatest savings from securitization in the form of capital cost savings. They would no longer be forced by regulatory capital requirements to hold capital equal to 7 percent of the loan, which is significantly higher than the actual, expected credit losses inherent in many types of high-quality loans.

For example, if a skilled intermediary creates a pool of car loans, its actual loan losses are likely to be under 1 percent of the principal amount of the loan over the life of the pool. If that intermediary sells the car loans to a special purpose vehicle, which in turn issues debt securities that are credit enhanced at a cost that reflects the actual credit risks inherent in the loans (a guaranty of 3 to 5 percent is more than sufficient for a high-quality pool of car loans), it can save significant equity capital costs.*

Of course, the fact that the highest-quality loans can be securitized most cost effectively is of great concern to regulators. They rightly fear that the highest-quality loans will go outside the banking and thrift system, leaving the FDIC and the FSLIC guaranteeing the lower-quality loans. But other forces are pushing in the same direction, as I described in Part 1 of this book. Moreover, whether bank and thrift regulators like it or not, credit securitization can be used by nonbanks to gain

---

*In classic corporate finance theory (i.e., Miller-Modigliani) selling high-quality assets raises the costs of equity. However, in a securitized credit transaction the selling institution, even for high-quality assets, sells more risks than benefits because the value added from the process permits it. No one has yet begun to deal with the implications of securitized credit on theoretical cost of equity calculations or classic corporate finance theory.

a share of high-quality assets, which will have the same effect. The more capital pressure regulators put on banks, the more high-quality assets will bypass the banking system through credit securitization. It is precisely because credit securitization accelerates the flight of high-quality assets that we must address the regulatory issues as soon as possible. As the technology becomes more and more efficient and effective, the high-quality assets will leave banks faster and faster.

In addition to the economic advantages of credit securitization, there are other advantages to the issuing institution. For example, the issuing institution gains access to a new funding source. Some institutions, such as GMAC, issue in such volume that they get significant benefits from using new instruments to tap new markets. Other institutions with severe credit problems may not even be able to raise money conventionally, while they can securitize their assets. Moreover, credit securitization enables the issuing institution to eliminate any interest rate risk it might incur by keeping the asset on its balance sheet. Many financial institutions are mismatched, and securitization can become a cost-effective way of neutralizing the interest rate risk of having fixed-rate loans that are funded with floating-rate deposits or liabilities. Finally, the issuing institution is expanding the total volume of business it can do with borrowers, since capital becomes less of a constraint on growth.

A final potential benefit to the issuing institution has not yet been tapped. Since credit securitization can free an institution from the constraints of its own balance sheet, many institutions could create new products. For example, U.S. commercial banks do not generally offer small businesses fixed-rate, medium-term loans; when they do, they charge borrowers very high rates. If banks can securitize these loans and transfer the interest rate risk, they may be able to create a product the borrower needs, charge a lower interest rate, and still earn substantial returns without taking any interest rate risk.

Despite all these advantages to the issuing intermediary, many bankers still dislike this technology—perhaps because it threatens their traditional way of operating. However, as will be explained in the rest of the book, I believe that bankers should embrace securitized credit because it could be pivotal in working their way through the challenges they now face.

Benefits to Investment Banks

While the issuing intermediaries can capture the bulk of the benefits of securitizing credits, the investment banks that structure and underwrite the securities also have great incentives to play this game. I have already mentioned the chief incentive: that they can earn underwriting fees and trading profits by financing borrowing activity in which they were not previously involved. For example, we estimate that investment banks have earned over $10 billion in revenue from issuing, structuring, and trading mortgage-backed securities during the 1980s. This is in a market—residential mortgages—where investment bankers played no significant role prior to the mid-1970s. The more loans that are securitized, the better it is for securities firms almost by definition. It is no surprise that the investment banks, particularly First Boston and Salomon, have been the driving force behind the rapid evolution of the securitized credit technology.

Benefits to Guarantors of Credit Risk

Guarantors who have the skills to assess credit risks have the opportunity to charge fees greater than expected losses without actually having to extend loans. The primary guarantors of credit risk (excluding the federal government, which is the real guarantor behind most mortgage debt that is securitized) are foreign commercial banks and special purpose insurance companies. As yet, this is an underdeveloped industry. As I will describe later on, the future regulation and economics of the credit enhancement industry are still very uncertain.

Benefits to Borrowers

In the short term the underlying borrowers reap few economic benefits from securitization. In fact, borrowers are often unaware that their loans have been securitized. In the early stages of securitization lenders have wanted to retain the savings from securitization for themselves. However, as more and more credit is securitized, competition will eventually force lenders to share the savings from securitization with borrowers, and then borrowers will be able to borrow money more cheaply. The real cost of borrowing could finally fall as much as 1 percent or more for many types of credit. That would benefit many a great deal.

Borrowers do benefit today from the increasing availability of credit on terms that lenders would not provide if they were forced to put the loans on their own balance sheets. This effect is most apparent with fixed-rate mortgage debt, which consumers greatly prefer over floating-rate debt. Many lenders are reluctant to extend fixed-rate debt on their own balance sheets—particularly given their experience in the early 1980s when the rates they paid on deposits rose rapidly, with short-term rates, while yields on their mortgage portfolios remained constant. Through mortgage-backed securities lenders can now extend fixed-rate mortgage debt without taking any interest-rate risk themselves. As a result, many more borrowers have access to fixed-rate mortgage debt than they would otherwise.

POTENTIAL IMPROVEMENTS IN THE
SOUNDNESS OF THE SYSTEM

Many regulators and observers have watched securitized credit grow and have heard all these arguments, but they remain very skeptical about this new technology. Indeed, they fear it can make a bad situation worse.

They rightly cite the Equity Programs Investment Corporation (EPIC) transaction of 1985 as an example of how a poorly underwritten securitized credit transaction can get into trouble. In that transaction a private mortgage-backed security, which was based on a pool of mortgages on builders' homes and was credit enhanced by a syndicate of mortgage insurance companies, went into default. The insurance companies sustained large losses (the principal guarantor, the Ticor Mortgage Insurance Company, is now bankrupt and is being liquidated), the underwriters' reputations were tarnished, and investors faced an immediate loss of liquidity on these securities and potentially sizeable losses on their principal. It will take years before the actual losses to all parties are known. If too many deals are poorly underwritten and if large defaults and losses result, this promising new technology could, at worst, hasten a credit collapse.

On the other hand, assuming that sufficient controls can be put in place and that the necessary infrastructure can be built, securitized credit offers four important advantages over traditional lending that will increase the soundness of credit extension. First, it ensures better credit underwriting. Second, it provides for better credit risk diversification. Third, it makes assets more liquid. Fourth, it transfers interest-rate risk to players who are better equipped to handle it than banks are. Let me review these benefits one at a time now; as I go, I will point to the kinds of safeguards that would be needed to realize each one.

A first advantage of securitized credit over traditional lending, from a soundness point of view, is that it should only be possible to securitize loans in which the *credit underwriting* is sound—that is, where the price charged for taking credit risk is more than the expected credit losses.

In the securitized credit process, *three* parties, rather than one, concern themselves with credit quality. In addition to the originators, the outside credit enhancer reviews the credit assessment skills, servicing capacity, and documentation of the originating institution before agreeing to participate. Credit enhancers are far less likely to have community or customer class biases than local commercial banks who tend to be overly optimistic about the health of the local or regional economy or the credit worthiness of a local borrower. Further, credit enhancers should have strong economic incentives to work with originating institutions to improve originators' credit skills. An additional incentive to judge credit quality correctly comes from the rating agency that looks over the shoulders of both the originator and the enhancer (Exhibit 6–5). Weak creditors will either have to improve their credit skills or be foreclosed from being able to securitize their loans. The net result is that credit underwriting through credit securitization is already far sounder than under the traditional system; it could be sounder

EXHIBIT 6–5
Credit Risk Diversification

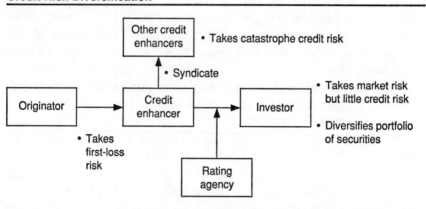

still if more safeguards were built into the system. Of the over 1,000 securitized credit issues done so far, only one, the EPIC transaction, has yet gone sour.

One major factor essential to making this new system sound is to ensure that the originator of the securitized credit transaction should retain at least the expected loss on the securitized loans and that the originator has the capacity to make good on its guarantee. The system will not work unless the loan originator is motivated to underwrite the credit properly and to service the underlying loans.

The major reason the mortgage insurance industry (not just Ticor Mortgage, which ensured EPIC) is in trouble is that mortgage insurers, rather than originators, insure the first loss. Most of the mortgage insurance industry has been based upon insuring borrowers' down payments, thus allowing borrowers to apply for mortgages that cover 90 percent, rather than 80 percent, of the purchase price of their homes. The originating banks, because they are not themselves exposed to first loss, have been less careful than they should in qualifying borrowers. In effect, they "pushed the bad paper downstream." Since inflation no longer bails out bad mortgage loans, most mortgage insurance companies have begun to experience high losses relative to their reserves.

To ensure the soundness of a securitized credit transaction, I believe the originator needs to guarantee at least two or three times the expected credit loss on the asset. For example, if well-underwritten automobile loans have an expected loss of .9 percent of the loan portfolio over the expected life of the asset, a first-loss guarantee by the originator of 3 percent would provide three and one-half times the expected loss. A second loss, "catastrophe" insurance guarantee of 6 percent by a credit insurance company, would involve very little risk. An insurance company could operate at such leverage (in this example 20 to 1) because the insurance company would benefit from diversification of risks—as well as the "deductible" protection provided by the first-loss guarantee of the originator. In this theoretical example the total capital being used would be only 3.3 percent of the loan (assuming the originator keeps dollar-for-dollar reserves for its first-loss guarantee). But the total protection to the investor from default would be 9 percent, or over 11 times the expected losses from the automobile loans. In contrast, the typical bank today has only 7.3 percent of capital protection (i.e., equity plus reserves). Thus, properly managed, the securitization process would provide better protection to investors, with less capital, and without government guarantees of deposits.

The need for a first-loss guarantee is a problem for banks, since current rules require any bank that guarantees the first loss on a loan to maintain capital as if it had kept the loan on its balance sheet. Fortunately there are certain exceptions and some techniques that give banks a limited ability to avoid this problem on certain classes of loans (such as mortgages and credit cards).

A second advantage of securitized credit over traditional lending is that it leads to *better diversification of credit risk*. Theoretically, a bank's loan portfolio should be a good diversifier of credit risk, but experience has proven this theory false. In fact, as we saw in Chapter 4, the traditional credit system has led to geographic concentrations of credit risk and credit losses. It would have to. Most banks originate most of their loans wherever they happen to be located. Thus, most banks in Oklahoma have loan portfolios filled with loans to independent oil producers, real estate developers, and farmers—partly because they were overoptimistic about the health of the local economy, and partly because they had few other lending opportunities. It is not surprising, therefore, that banks in the West North Central and West South Central charged off loans at a rate of about twice the national average in 1986, while banks in New England and the Middle Atlantic states have been experiencing only marginal charge-offs.

Credit securitization allows this credit risk to be diversified. While expected losses are retained by the originator, "catastrophe" credit risk is placed with a credit enhancer, and this in turn is usually syndicated to other credit enhancers. In the process "catastrophe" credit risk is spread from the originating institution to credit enhancers, with any residual risk borne by investors, who further spread the risk by diversifying their portfolios. If this system had been in place in the early 1980s, it would have prevented the kind of regional concentration of credit charge-offs we are seeing now.

The third dimension in which securitized credit adds to soundness relative to traditional lending is *liquidity*. The traditional lending technology produces illiquid assets. Banks make few short-term, self-liquidating loans these days. There is no secondary market for most loans, with the exception of the whole loan mortgage market and short-term loans to large corporations. Once a loan is made to a borrower, the bank has limited ability to convert that loan back to cash until the borrower repays the bank. This means that banks can do little to adjust their loan portfolios for changing interest rates or local market conditions. Since economic volatility has become a way of life, this lack of liquidity makes banks more vulnerable than they need to be.

In contrast, securities are liquid. If a commercial bank had more such assets, its balance sheet would be far more liquid than at present. As a result, it could adjust its portfolio much more quickly to changing conditions. Other investors can, of course, either hold or sell credit securities just like any other security in their portfolios—and as I have pointed out before, this is one reason (coupled with loan sales) why the overall cost of credit extension is lower under securitized credit than traditional lending.

The fourth comparison I want to make between the traditional credit system and securitized credit is in terms of *interest-rate risk*. In 1980 interest-sensitive deposits comprised about

50 percent of total bank liabilities; today that figure is more like 75 percent. A good portion of the industry has responded very intelligently to the increasing market rate sensitivity of the liability side of their balance sheets by intelligent interest-rate risk management.

On the other hand, as was pointed out in Chapter 4, many other banks and thrifts have begun to make large interest-rate bets. Because floating rates and assets have relatively low yields, many banks and thrifts have made two different types of interest-rate bets: first, discretionary bets involving fixed-rate investments in the investment portfolio and, second, fixed-rate assets generated in the course of doing banking business, such as the credit card book and the auto loan book on the consumer side. As highly leveraged institutions, banks are poorly structured to take significant interest-rate risk. Even modest mismatches can lead to significant losses. I believe that a great many banks and thrifts are now making large interest-rate bets by playing the yield curve—that is, by raising interest-sensitive deposits and investing them in fixed-rate investments.

By offering securitized credit, banks and thrifts could continue to offer fixed-rate loans to customers while avoiding interest-rate bets. Through securitized credit, fixed-rate interest risk would be transferred to the end investor, who is far better structured to take that risk. For example, pension funds and mutual funds are not leveraged institutions; they are simply pass-through vehicles for underlying investors. They are properly structured and managed to take market risk; indeed, that is one of their basic functions for the underlying investors they represent.

While these benefits of securitization are very important, they are by no means guaranteed. The new technology will not evolve toward soundness all by itself, no matter how many investment bankers, investors, and borrowers want it to. Congress and regulators must take some proactive steps to create an environment that will shape the development of securitized credit into a sounder system. That means first correcting some problems we have now. But before describing those regulatory issues, we need to explore how the new technology can be used to rethink the bank.

CHAPTER 7

BREAKING UP THE BANK: A NEW MODEL

In Chapter 3 I pointed out that one effective method of correcting industry overcapacity is to disaggregate and restructure integrated suppliers. I also noted that the bundled banking model makes disaggregation particularly difficult in this industry. But here, the securitized credit technology can play a facilitating role in the needed restructuring of banks. It suggests a new, unbundled model for banking that could enable us to break away from the traditional banking business system that was appropriate 700 years ago in medieval Europe but is less and less so today.

If we redesign banks to participate fully in the securitized credit technology, we can give the public the benefits of competition without relying on massive government subsidies. We can both benefit the banks themselves and improve the efficiency, the effectiveness, and the soundness of the financial system as a whole. And we can do it while preserving the value that the banking and thrift industries add to their existing customer bases.

How do we accomplish all of this?

The task is conceptually simple. We must use the new securitized credit technology to unbundle, or break apart, the bank into its component functions so that each function can be performed by whichever players are most capable of delivering the best service at the best price. Specifically, this means separating deposit taking from credit risk taking (and from the other risks, other functions, and other services performed by a bank as well). The objective would be to redesign banks so that each customer pays for the full costs of the explicit, discrete services he or she uses without cross-subsidizing others or being cross-subsidized by others.

In other words, each customer should pay for, and receive, fair value. Depositors should pay for the full costs of the payment system and federal deposit insurance without being subsidized by borrowers or other bank customers. Borrowers should pay for the full costs of their specific borrowing needs without subsidy from the government, other borrowers, or depositors and, most especially, without putting depositors' funds at risk.

All this can be done using credit securitization, because this technology allows for a variety of discrete, functional roles. The bank that reorganizes around these roles will become unbundled. Then, it can assess its cost effectiveness in each role and eliminate through sale or shutdown any function that other players, with better skill, are performing more cost-effectively. In this way, overall industry overcapacity, which is the core problem of the banking and thrift industries, would be reduced and the system would become more efficient. Once the low value-added functions or services are either spun-off or simply eliminated, the high value-added component parts of the bank can be reassembled into a new, value-based financial institution. This new value-based financial institution would no longer have the *internal* structure of a bank as we know banks today.

However, in many, many cases, this institution would look very familiar *to its customers.* Most banks' best skills today are in serving their individual, small business, and corporate customers. Therefore, most institutions will probably see their best opportunities to add value in roles that are based on serving customers. There is room for thousands of institutions devoted to customer service.

Most readers undoubtedly find these suggestions radical. A host of questions immediately come to mind. The first, most general one is: How would this model work?

THE NEW MODEL

As described in the Technical Note at the end of the book, a wide variety of proposals have been made in the last few years for reform of banking regulation. Many of these proposals are now converging, and the model I am proposing draws on the ideas of a large number of others. In particular, the model I am advocating is closest to proposals made by Robert Litan of the Brookings Institute. What is new about the model I'm proposing is that it is based upon the widespread application of the securitized credit technology; the full disaggregation of the functions now called "banking" into discrete businesses; and the reliance on competition, technology, and the marketplace, rather than regulation, to redefine the business of banking.

Under this new model an institution would only perform those functions in which it enjoyed a competitive advantage. In the traditional model every bank has performed nearly every function, whether it was good at that function or not. For example, as long as the only way to fund a loan is by raising deposits, banks with lending skills need to raise deposits even if they are not terribly skilled at deposit taking or if their only deposit sources are relatively very expensive. Similarly, banks with strong deposit gathering skills but weak lending skills still have to do something with the deposits once they are raised; these institutions are the source of the massive credit problems in the system today.

Under the new model some institutions would focus on lending; in many cases they would concentrate only on certain types of loans. Others would focus on depositors. Still others would focus on servicing roles, or credit insurance roles, or investment banking roles. Any single institution could perform more than one of these roles, depending on where it was able to add value. But each role would be a discrete business, managed through a holding company.

Holding companies would be allowed to own both depository institutions and a wide variety of other companies including finance companies (to hold nonsecuritized loans), securities affiliates, credit-risk insurance companies, or even industrial companies. The holding company would be a source of financial strength, and it would still be possible to gain the benefits of synergy between functions through management, but the risks and economics of each subsidiary would be kept separate. Only one type of subsidiary—the depository institution—would be protected by federal guarantees. Despite the evils of federal guarantees I have already described, we must have a *"risk-free" depository institution*, which I will talk more about in a moment. What would save the new system from the negative aspects of federal guarantees is that protection would be limited to deposits (and, by extension, payments). The government would need to be prepared to allow any subsidiary *other than* a "risk-free" insured depository to fail. Thus, the financial discipline of the nondepository subsidiaries would be provided by the marketplace, since lenders and investors would have neither implicit nor explicit government guarantees of their risks. Now, let us talk about why *selective* government guarantees make sense.

I can not think of a feasible alternative to government guarantees on the deposit side. Even though it is clear that the combination of deposit insurance and competition is at the core of our credit problems today, we obviously need government deposit insurance. That insurance is the only reason why we have been able to avoid bank panics for the last 50 years.

Similar issues surround our payment system. The failure of any large bank, or securities firm, is unthinkable because the payment system effectively links every large, worldwide player together through counterparty risk. For example, whenever a trade between two institutions is completed there is a lag between when the trade is made and when the cash exchange takes place between the counterparties to the transaction. Given the enormous volumes being traded today, and the enormous amount of payments that result, the cross-institution exposures are enormous. Thus, if even one major institution were allowed to fail, its defaults on payments would cause other institutions to default in "daisy chain" fashion, until the entire system failed. This was why Continental Illinois could not fail in 1982. It is why major securities firms, even though their liabilities are not guaranteed by the government, cannot be allowed to fail. The federal government today, through the Federal Reserve, has to protect not only depositors in failed banks, but also the entire worldwide financial system economy, insofar as that economy is linked into the payment system. In other words, the federal government winds up absorbing the eventual consequences of bad risk taking by any very large bank or securities firm—whether the risk involves LDC lending, interest-rate betting, or trading decisions.

I believe we can address both sets of issues, without encouraging imprudent lending or risk taking, by creating a largely risk-free depository institution and payment system.* The term "risk free" is a misnomer; what is actually being proposed is a "low-risk" depository institution. But the term "risk free" better captures the spirit of what I'm talking about. Therefore, the term "risk free," with quotes around it, will be used in this book to describe a system where federally insured depositories would only be allowed to take very modest risks. In this system the institution taking deposits insured by the government would be allowed to invest those funds only in instruments with no significant credit risk (such as federal government obligations or securities rated AA or better) and no significant interest-rate risk (such as floating-rate risk or short-term bonds and notes). These investment restrictions would be similar to the restrictions contained in the prospectuses of money market mutual funds. Such investment limitations would protect the government from significant risk-related losses, and deposit insurance premiums would be more than adequate to protect against the occasional bank that failed due to operating losses, management fraud, or other malfeasance.

Such "risk-free" depository institutions would begin to make the payment system more safe, if they were the only institutions empowered to make payments larger than, for example, $20 million per day. Under such a system, an institution taking credit risks or a securities firm taking trading risks would either have to keep enough cash in a "risk-free" depository to settle its transactions daily or set up a regulated, "risk-free" depository of its own and run it as a separate subsidiary.

Of course, deposits in the risk-free deposit and payment

---

*The notion of "risk-free" (or "fail-safe") depository institution has only entered the public debate in the last few years. Several other proponents who have advocated some form of "risk-free" depository include Litan, Kareken, Lawrence, and Angermueller. Critics include Bentson and Kaufman. The proposal in this book differs from others in that it is tied to credit securitization and the continuation of federal deposit insurance of "low-risk" depository institutions. See the Technical Note at the end of the book.

system would earn low returns compared to alternative money market instruments. This would serve to increase the flow of funds through nondepository channels (e.g., money market mutual funds, bond funds) and reduce the flow of funds through depository channels as investors sought higher returns than were available from "risk-free" depositories.

On the lending side, for all the reasons I have already explained, the new system should place the full burden of risk on the lending institution, its business partners, and its investors. That is, credit risk and interest-rate risk would be borne by independent, nondepository institutions (which would include nondepository subsidiaries of holding companies that also own depository institutions). For nonsecuritized loans, credit and interest-rate risk would be absorbed by finance companies. For securitized loans, these risks would be absorbed by different parties. First loss (i.e., "expected" credit losses) would be absorbed by the reserves of special purpose subsidiaries of the holding company, and second loss (i.e., "catastrophe" credit losses) would be absorbed by credit enhancers (e.g., credit-risk monoline insurance companies, full-line insurance companies, non-U.S. banks). Interest-rate risk of securitized loans would be taken either by the end investors in the securities or by institutions that have sufficient private capital and skill to manage that risk.

The subsidiaries taking credit risk and interest-rate risk would not be entitled to federal insurance and therefore would depend for funds on the issuance of securities such as commercial paper and or bonds to investors. These investors demand high-quality financial skills, adequate equity capital protection, and a good return. The government would no longer subsidize lending spreads, so spreads on high-risk loans would rise until they reflected the underlying credit risk of the loans. Conversely, over time, the efficiencies of the new technology would lower the costs of loans with low credit risk.

Of course, nonbank holding companies have always relied on the discipline of the marketplace, and their experience argues in its favor. Numerous large and mid-size bank holding companies have had deep troubles and required massive government assistance, but nonbank financial holding companies have generally been pillars of financial strength. Some good examples are American Express, General Electric Credit Corporation, Ford Motor Credit, and IBM Credit. Furthermore, investment banks routinely take and manage significant interest-rate risk without relying on government guarantees.

Let me summarize: Under this model credit risk and interest-rate risk would still exist, but they would largely by-pass the depository system, and they would affect the payment system far less than they do now. In every function, protected or not, success would flow to the institutions that provide their customers with better value relative to competitors. Let us now see what that would entail—first for credit, then for deposit taking.

VALUE-BASED CREDIT EXTENSION

What the borrower *wants* from a lender is credit with the best terms and availability at the best price. But the borrower also *needs* discipline from a lender who looks skeptically at the borrower's ability to repay. As I have already said, the biggest problem of the existing banking system is that uneconomic credit is currently being extended (that is, loans are being made whose expected credit losses exceed expected returns). Making bad loans benefits no one, particularly the borrower. Just ask midwestern farmers or independent oil producers in the Southwest who found themselves overextended.

Clearly, any new financial model must do a better job of ensuring that loans are properly underwritten. The proposed model does that, because it is based on structured securitized credit. As described in the last chapter, this technology promises better credit underwriting because it allows for objective credit evaluation by disinterested outsiders, like conduits, credit enhancers, and rating agencies, who have an economic stake in sound credit underwriting. What is more, this technology would be much less expensive in terms of capital requirements than the current traditional credit system.

What would be the capital savings? They would vary,

since the amount of capital required from originators and credit enhancers to protect investors from default would depend upon the class of asset being securitized. Credit risks and prepayment risks vary significantly depending upon the actual loan, or portfolio of loans, being securitized (e.g., the credit worthiness of the particular borrowers, the specific lending terms, and the collateral securing the loans). In the automobile loan example in Chapter 6, however, we saw significant capital savings with better protection for investors. Done properly, I would expect every securitized credit transaction to provide better protection to investors, with better matching of capital to the specific risks in the loans, and without government guarantees of deposits.

Clearly, a new financial system based on this technology would add tremendous value to all participants. The next question is: Who specifically would provide what kind of value, and how would they profit from their activities?

The participant who originates the credit directly from the end borrower would provide the most value both by tailoring the terms and availability of the credit to the circumstances and the ability of the borrower to pay *and* by absorbing the first loss. To do these things well the originator must have both customer knowledge and credit skills (knowledge of collateral, underwriting skill, collections skill). The value added by these skills is particularly large in the individual, small business, and mid-sized company markets—the core of the customer base of most banks.

Moreover, these skills will remain valuable as the system evolves. A high degree of tailoring will always be needed, despite the standardization associated with credit securitization. For example, at least 25 varieties of standardized mortgages are being securitized, and mortgage lending is always tailored to the estimated value of the property and the borrower's ability to service the debt. In fact, one proof of the enduring value of origination is the literally thousands of small mortgage bankers who still thrive in the very large securitized mortgage business. Similarly, as I noted in Chapter 6, the originator should always have to absorb the expected credit losses from lending money, despite the improvements in underwriting that securitization would enforce. No other party can have as good a knowledge of the quality of the credit being extended as does the originator. No other party can therefore be expected to absorb the first loss.

The profit an originator can earn will vary with the kind of asset. In mortgage banking, for example, the originator generally earns a *point* (1 percent of the value of the mortgage) plus the net present value of the expected income from servicing the loans. Many originators work on a "servicing released" basis, whereby they sell the servicing rights to another servicer, for an additional point of revenue. The costs of origination usually exceed 1 point, but the combined revenues from origination and servicing make this a profitable business indeed for the mortgage banks (Exhibit 7–1).

In car loans—at least in those securitized by the General Motors Acceptance Corporation—the value added in origination is almost completely captured by the originator. In most of the securitized deals GMAC has done, GMAC has captured almost

EXHIBIT 7–1
Estimated Industry Profits—Mortgage Organization, 1986 ($Billions)

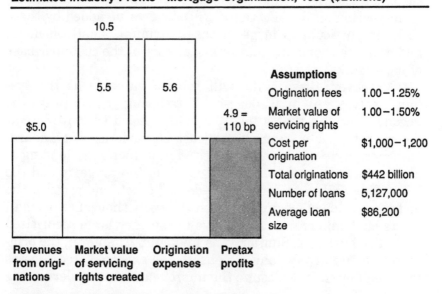

Assumptions	
Origination fees	1.00–1.25%
Market value of servicing rights	1.00–1.50%
Cost per origination	$1,000–1,200
Total originations	$442 billion
Number of loans	5,127,000
Average loan size	$86,200

Revenues from originations: $5.0
Market value of servicing rights created: 5.5 (10.5)
Origination expenses: 5.6 (4.9 = 110 bp)
Pretax profits

Sources: HUD; Mortgage Bankers Association; McKinsey analysis

all of its original spread on the loan. We estimate that its cash funding costs on the securitized transaction have only been .15 to .20 basis points above what it would have paid if it had issued debt that match funded its loans. Moreover, on an all-in basis, including equity costs, we estimate that GMAC realized substantial savings—on the order of 100 basis points.

To a certain extent, the profit an originator can earn will also vary with its bargaining power, which in many cases will be synonymous with size. Structurers and credit enhancers will find larger packages of loans more attractive and will accept lower spreads for supplying their functional skills. For this reason, smaller originators will need to work—and share some of their profits with—conduits, who will pool loans together to gain bargaining power relative to structurers and credit enhancers.

Of course, substantial profits will also be earned throughout the securitized credit business system by the players with the right skills and the right scale. As I have suggested, most banks are probably best prepared to play the origination role, with or without the help of a conduit, although many banks will also play a strong servicing role. Some banks may choose to play in other functional areas—but they should do so *after* reflecting on the fact that structuring, credit enhancement, placing, trading, and some forms of servicing lend themselves to economies of scale and benefit from specialization. Since the key to success in these specialized businesses will be relative value added versus all other competitors, we would expect to see fewer, larger competitors in these functions than in origination. Some of these large competitors would be companies that serve as "shared utilities" for others.

VALUE-ADDED DEPOSIT TAKING

Institutions deliver value to depositors by providing interest on the deposits, convenience, safety, and third-party payment services. Providing deposit services is the core of the charter of banks worldwide and the primary role of this country's 42,000-odd commercial bank branches. Customers deposit and withdraw cash frequently and therefore greatly value the convenience of a branch for these services. In contrast, customers apply for loans infrequently and are willing to travel greater distances to borrow; therefore, branch convenience is not terribly important in borrowing. For most institutions deposit services are an expensive business. In addition to branch costs, deposit servicing requires enormous investment in paper handling, computer processing, and customer service (e.g., inquiries). All told, we at McKinsey estimate that roughly half of all the noninterest expenses of banks are related to deposit taking (e.g., approximately $50 billion of expenses).

The chief advantage of the model being proposed is that it would allow depository institutions to continue to add value as depositories with government protection but without the huge government subsidies that are needed now to protect depositors against bad lending decisions. Depositors have every right to expect a safe depository, and the payment and deposit system must be protected from default for all the reasons outlined earlier in this chapter. This system would provide that protection at much lower cost than we currently incur, because the institution holding the deposits would be much less risky. The cost of the current system stems from the fact that, today, banks are "blind pools" of risks—and some of those risks are uneconomic. If we move to "risk-free" depositories, government deposit insurance can be provided economically and without subsidy.

A second advantage is that it would tend to make the deposit servicing business more cost-effective, by forcing the consolidation of deposit taking functions until they reached an economic size. Today many banks and thrifts either have low skills in deposit taking or are the wrong size to be effective depositories. These very banks often take excessive credit or interest-rate risk to mask the inefficiencies of deposit taking. For example, we estimate that a single branch bank with $25 million of deposits may incur noninterest expenses, as a percentage of deposits, of 4 percent. In contrast, a $100 million single-branch bank may incur noninterest expenses, as a percentage of deposits, of only 2 to 2.5 percent. It is not surprising that a very large number of very small banks today are losing money due to bad credit decisions. If we ever again are exposed to high interest rates or an inverted yield curve, the number of small institutions losing money could reach staggeringly large levels. Many of these banks would likely consolidate into more cost-effective, more value-based, "risk-free" depositories if the model being proposed were adopted. However, any smaller institution that could add sufficient value to its customers could obviously remain independent.

The consolidation need not reduce the number of depository locations, since local convenience is important to depositors. Rather, I would foresee a consolidation of back-office activities, with several small banks becoming branches of a new holding company. This trend would be a continuation of the kind of growth among regional banks we have seen in the last few years. They are continuing to provide locally based service while achieving scale economics behind the scenes—and they have done very well.

The economics of a "risk-free" depository could be relatively attractive. It would take only core, below-market-rate deposits, such as demand deposits, savings accounts, and small money market accounts. It would not take large money market deposits; these would be uneconomic for the "risk-free" depository because it would only be allowed to invest in very-high-quality assets, which would yield less than the cost of large money market deposits on the open market. Thus, the "risk-free" depository's only customers would be those individuals and companies who were willing to pay for the value of having a "risk-free" depository—either by accepting a below-market rate of interest on their deposits or by paying substantial service fees. In addition to retail and wholesale payment services, demand deposits, and retail savings deposits, these institutions could also offer wholesale cash management services, safekeeping and custody services, and the other operating services now offered by a bank.

Moreover, since these institutions would incur little risk, they would require little capital and therefore earn relatively attractive returns (Exhibit 7-2). The example shown in the

EXHIBIT 7–2
Risk-Free Depository ($Millions)*

Assets		Liabilities		Income and Expenses	
T-bills (6.5%)	$20	Consumer money market (5%)	$70	Deposit fees	$0.7
				Interest income	7.3
Securitized assets (7.5%)	80	Demand deposits (0%)	26	Operating income	8.0
	$100	Equity	4	Interest expense	3.5
			$100	Net interest revenue	4.5
				Operating expense	3.0
				Pretax income	$1.5
				Pretax ROE	37.5%

*There is room for 1,000 to 1,500 of this risk-free depository.

exhibit assumes that 20 percent of the institution's assets would be held in reserves at the Federal Reserve earning interest at the Treasury bill rate. If required reserves were noninterest bearing (as they are today), then rates paid by depositors would have to be less, or the fees paid by them would have to be higher, or both, to achieve these same economics. More will be said about this issue in the next chapter.

CHAPTER 8

LEGISLATIVE CHANGE AND REGULATORY ACTION

It is one thing to talk about a model. It is another thing to talk about making that model an operating reality. The model I have described implies enormous changes. Value conscious customers, competition, technology, and economic pressures are already moving the system in the proposed direction, but to ensure its soundness we will also need fundamental changes in the laws and regulations that govern our depository institutions—as well as a great deal of time. The truth is, it took us years to get the system into its present dismal shape, and it will take years to make the system whole again.

Before we redesign our existing regulatory and legislative framework we need to understand why it is ineffective as it stands. Then we need to adjust it carefully to correct our existing credit problems, while preserving the healthy parts of our current credit system. Finally, we should rewrite our regulations and laws to encourage the development of the industry on the model described in the last chapter.

EXISTING SYSTEM OUTMODED

I described in Part 1 how we introduced intense competition into our financial system without changing the underlying regulatory framework. I have already pointed out the connection between our regulatory safety nets and our credit problems. But there are other reasons why the existing framework is wrong for today's financial environment. First, new financial services

technologies—particularly the securitized credit technology—
are making many of the existing regulations and laws ineffective; laws designed for horses and buggies, to make an analogy to transportation, have little application to automobiles.
Second, our regulations are designed for separate, discrete
industries, while competition has caused our historic industry
definitions to overlap; as a result, different players are now,
incongruously, being regulated differently in the same functional activity. Third, our regulatory structure and political system do not give our regulators the tools they need to deal with
incompetent participants.

Let's look at these reasons one at a time.

1. *Technology is making laws and regulations ineffective.*
In mid-1987 the Senate Banking Committee held hearings on
the impact of technology on regulation. The consistent theme
of both regulators and outside experts was that our regulatory
structure for financial institutions had become outdated due to
new technology and financial innovation. New financial capabilities exist today that carry a host of new risks. Those risks
are not addressed by the old regulatory structure, and they lead
to problems that have to be addressed on the spot by whatever
regulator or court sees them first.

Securitized credit technology, for example, has grown up
around the laws and regulations that govern banks, thrifts,
securities firms, and insurance companies—but it contains
numerous uncovered risks. One has come to light in the wake
of the failed EPIC transaction. Ticor Mortgage, the lead credit
insurance company, has undergone bankruptcy and liquidation
as a result of the EPIC transaction. But a host of mortgages
and mortgage-backed securities *outside* the EPIC deal, which
had also been insured by Ticor, have been affected. Ticor Mortgage was overseen by California insurance regulators. Given
the importance of credit enhancement to the securitized credit
business system, and given the national implications of decisions on liquidation and division of the proceeds, it seems that
the rules governing credit enhancement should be set by national, rather than state, regulation.

Another risk of securitized credit is that the sale of assets
to a special purpose vehicle could be challenged in bankruptcy

court. If a contract is judged not to constitute a "true sale," the assets supposedly protected for a particular deal could be taken back—not only destroying an otherwise soundly structured deal, but also shaking the faith of the public and all players in this promising new technology. While most lawyers involved do not believe such challenges could succeed, the success or uncertainty created by otherwise "impossible" lawsuits in Texas courts (e.g., the Pennzoil-Texaco battle and the Hunt brothers versus banks trying to collect on defaulted loans) at least raise the possibility that such a lawsuit could succeed.

In the wake of the October 1987 stock market crash, we saw similar problems related to other new technologies, such as stock futures trading. Again, laws and regulations exist *around* these technologies, overseen by the Securities Exchange Commission (SEC), the Federal Commodity Trade Commission, and the various exchanges. But margin requirements that were set years ago to enforce prudence in commodities trading proved inadequate when the futures markets were used to leverage bets on the stock market to incredible levels.

2. *Industries are increasingly overlapping.* While technology is making some regulations obsolete, aggressive players are using smart lawyers to bypass others. By identifying the right loopholes many players have been able to offer financial services that look remarkably like services regulation forbids them to offer.

Consider, for example, the overlaps that virtually negate Glass-Steagall, the law separating banking from securities. New York money center banks engage in loan sales (which look like commercial paper) and discount brokerage (which often looks like full-service retail brokerage). They underwrite their own securitized credit transactions in the same syndicate as a normal investment bank, privately place huge debt transactions to a wide variety of institutional investors, sell mutual funds but do not sponsor them, and act as full-line securities firms all around the world, except in New York. Meanwhile, securities firms sponsor mutual funds with check writing privileges, trade foreign exchange, market home equity loans, and even provide bridge financing (taking enormous credit risk in the process) to close major corporate restructurings. The chief beneficiaries of the existing laws are: (1) the lawyers who ensure that the participants keep within the law but nevertheless function as if the laws separating banking from securities did not exist and (2) participants in particular niches who are protected by law from competition, such as salesmen of municipal revenue bonds. Hopefully, by the time this book is published, Glass-Steagall will have been rewritten.

But overlaps are not confined to Glass-Steagall issues. The credit extension function is regulated by the FDIC (for most small, state-chartered banks and mutual savings banks), by the Comptroller of the Currency (for national banks), by the Federal Reserve (for large bank holding companies), by the FSLIC (for the S&L industry), by the SEC (for securities firms), by state insurance regulators (for credit-guaranteeing insurance companies), and by private agencies, such as accountants, rating agencies, and the marketplace (for nonregulated players such as finance companies). The deposit taking function is regulated by the FDIC, the FSLIC, the SEC (for money market mutual funds), and the Federal Reserve (for the payment and money transfer system).

The functionality of the credit and deposit products offered by various players may be the same, but the regulations governing them, which are written by different groups, vary enormously. For example, a commercial bank is limited to lending no more than 10 percent of its capital; in contrast, several investment banks have lent more than 50 percent of their capital in financing a single acquisition. A commercial bank taking a first loss guarantee of just 1 or 2 percent on a securitized credit transaction has to maintain as much capital as if it had kept the entire loan on its own books; a finance company only reports a similar guarantee as a contingent liability. The FDIC routinely takes over failing banks; the FSLIC (lacking the money to do otherwise) allows hopelessly insolvent thrifts to keep raising deposits. The list of regulatory anomalies could go on and on.

3. *A legislative and regulatory gridlock prevents regulation and law from adapting.* Because differences in regulation lead to different competitive advantages, the different participants all seek to maximize their own self-interest through their own personal lobbying and through their trade associations. This leads to a legislative gridlock that prevents movement on important changes in law. For example, one reason why the thrift industry issues described earlier in the book have not been addressed is that the thrift lobby is very powerful. For a long time thrift associations prevented the FSLIC from obtaining funds or dealing effectively with failed thrifts; they have recently begun to change their attitudes as their problems have become more visible. For its part, the Securities Industry Association has successfully held up Glass-Steagall law changes for years. And even commercial banks are divided among themselves, with small bankers often pitted against large bankers. Somehow the public interest gets lost in the debate.

Meanwhile, regulators are doing the best they can with the tools and funds they have available to them. The FSLIC can not, however, liquidate insolvent thrifts without money. It must use the money it has available just to keep the system operating. Our regulators need broad national support, including new financial support, to deal with the issues they face. Instead, they are under constant assault.

KEEPING THE PRESENT CREDIT SYSTEM FROM BREAKING DOWN

As I noted in Chapter 5, sooner or later some precipitating event will occur that will break the gridlock. Finally, an enraged public will give regulators the mandate they need to clean up the credit problems and unsound credit practices of U.S. depository institutions. We would be wise, however, not to wait for that event. If we start today, the cleanup will be expensive but manageable. If we wait, we will face additional expense and probably have to do the job in an atmosphere of panic, rather than in one merely of discomfort and displeasure.

The U.S. government should begin the cleanup by liquidating hopelessly insolvent thrifts in an orderly manner—and, as I have shown in Chapter 5, that will take a lot more cash than the FSLIC has available to it now. While some of the necessary money can come from the insurance premiums of solvent thrifts, I believe the FSLIC is going to have to turn to the federal government for bailout funds. As I said in Chapter 5, I estimate that some $50 billion to $100 billion will be needed. The Federal Home Loan Bank Board and FSLIC maintain, at least in public, that it would cost less—mostly because they only count the carrying costs needed to keep the system operating for the next two or three years and because they persist in thinking they can find buyers for insolvent thrifts without providing the full subsidy needed to compensate buyers for the risks they are taking on (a promulgation of the "greater fool" theory). But I can not be that optimistic. Overcapacity has greatly reduced the charter value of thrifts as vehicles, and bad loans will not miraculously get better. If anything, I expect the costs of liquidating insolvent thrifts to rise above the current (i.e., 1988) level, which is over 30 percent of assets.

The U.S. taxpayer is already on the hook for these losses in the thrift industry, since the full faith and credit of the U.S. government now stands behind the insurance funds. This is just as well, because major deposit defaults are one of the few ways we could guarantee a repeat of the Great Depression.

Compared to the government's annual budget of $1 trillion, the cash needed for orderly liquidation in insolvent thrifts is modest: $20 billion to $30 billion a year for three to five years would probably be enough; this would represent between 2 and 3 percent of the budget in any given year. Of course, the taxpayers' reaction to such an ongoing public bailout of private institutions would be negative, but there is really no escape. Time will not cure truly hopeless cases. The sooner we address the cost of liquidation, the lower the eventual costs will be. Thanks to the more conservative nature of commercial bank regulation, there are still enough resources in the commercial banking system and the FDIC to liquidate insolvent commercial banks routinely; no public bailout is yet needed in this sector (although that could change if we had a deep recession). Again, the faster we move here, the less expensive and painful the liquidation process will be.

The liquidation of insolvent institutions would, importantly, reduce overcapacity in the commercial banking and thrift industries, thus improving the health of the remaining institutions. This would help prevent the failure of even more thrifts and banks, which would avoid further government bailouts in the future.

Finally, U.S. bank and thrift regulators should be able to exercise stop-lending powers in advance of the actual insolvency of a bank or thrift. As the liquidation of insolvent banks and thrifts proceeds, it is important that the situation be actively managed so that new problem institutions do not emerge. Banks and thrifts with high charge-off rates and inadequate capital should be prevented from lending more money until they have brought in the necessary management skills and have been recapitalized. U.S. regulators should be empowered, either under their existing authority or through additional grants of power, as necessary, to impose a stop-lending rule whenever an institution crosses a predefined boundary line. For example, lending powers might be stopped when an institution's equity drops below 2 percent of loans and leases *and* its charge-off rates over an 18-month period are in the worst 20 percent of similar institutions. Lending would not be permitted again until the institution was recapitalized.

This one-time cleanup needs to begin as soon as possible. We should start with the worst cases and simply keep going until the problems are fixed.

BUILDING THE NEW REGULATORY MODEL

While economic forces and the securitized credit technology are encouraging the evolution of an unbundled banking system, proactive support from the government will make the evolution more effective, faster, and safer. Europe would have recovered anyway after the Second World War; the Marshall Plan made that recovery far faster than and more beneficial to both Europe and ourselves, because it provided support to a natural recovery process. But even with the Marshall Plan it took a decade for Europe to recover. Time will also be needed to heal the problems of our depository institutions. It will probably take two or three years just to design and put in place a new regulatory system and new financial system, and another three to five years before they are fully effective.

I believe that our regulators and legislators should work

together over the first couple of years of this period to take the following steps:

1. Rewrite holding company law to allow any financial or industrial institution to own any type of financial subsidiary and manage it through a financial holding company structure. Establish a single body of law and oversight mechanism for financial holding companies and their subsidiaries.

2. Rewrite regulation *by function*, rather than by industry, so that all independent subsidiaries pursuing the same business are subject to the same controls.

3. During this functional rewrite, work to foresee potential problems related to the new financial technologies—particularly securitized credit—and address them *proactively*.

4. Develop regulations that create "risk-free" depository institutions and encourage risk to migrate from them into other subsidiaries not protected by federal guarantees.

5. To the extent that "risk-free" depository institutions fall short of protecting the payment system, develop other approaches for doing so.

Let's now look at each of these steps more closely.

1. *Rewrite holding company law.* Today, some financial holding companies are regulated far more tightly than others. Bank holding companies, overseen by the Federal Reserve, are most tightly controlled. Nonbank financial holding companies are primarily regulated by private institutions like the Financial Accounting Standards Board, the stock exchanges, and the rating agencies, which the SEC has encouraged to grow.

I believe the SEC model of holding company regulation has been demonstrably superior to the bank holding company model in guaranteeing soundness. I further believe that the first step in rationalizing our regulatory system would be to provide consistent holding company regulation of all financial services. Since securitized credit technology is enabling us to unbundle deposit taking from credit extension, there is no reason why any institution, financial or industrial, should not be allowed to participate in any aspect of financial service—provided that risk-free deposits, guaranteed by the federal government, are kept separate.

Thus, any financial holding company should be permitted to own both depository institutions and a wide variety of other subsidiaries, including those engaged in all types of securities and insurance activities (particularly including credit insurance companies). There would be no distinction between a bank and a nonbank holding company. It would be possible for holding companies owning traditional securities or insurance companies to own depository institutions and for traditional bank holding companies to own securities and insurance companies.

2. *Regulate financial activities functionally.* Of course, more must be done at the regulatory level than provide for uniform holding company regulation. The next important step is for the government to regulate each financial function consistently for every player engaged in that function. To this end, regulation should mandate that separate functions of the securitized credit business system, as well as other financial activities, be performed by separate and independent subsidiaries (i.e., in regulatory parlance *firewalls*). Then the government should work to ensure that all the institutions facing the same risks are regulated equally. Clearly, several regulators should not regulate the same function in different industries. Rather, a single regulator should oversee the same function for all participants (Exhibit 8–1).

Consider, for example, how the functions of the securitized credit business system might be regulated. One regulator could oversee credit extension. Its charter would include such activities as insuring that terms and conditions are fully disclosed to borrowers (i.e., "truth in lending") and that originators of loans being securitized actually maintain the assets (i.e., possessed the capital and reserves) they are warranting to others. Another regulator could be responsible for the structuring function—ensuring, for example, that all the contracts used in securitizing credit were valid for legal and tax purposes. Another regulator could be responsible for the credit enhancement and credit insurance functions—ensuring, for example, that reserves are adequate for the risks being accepted and that proper procedures and processes are in place. Another regulator could ensure that the placing and trading functions are

EXHIBIT 8–1
Move to Functional Rather than Industry Regulation

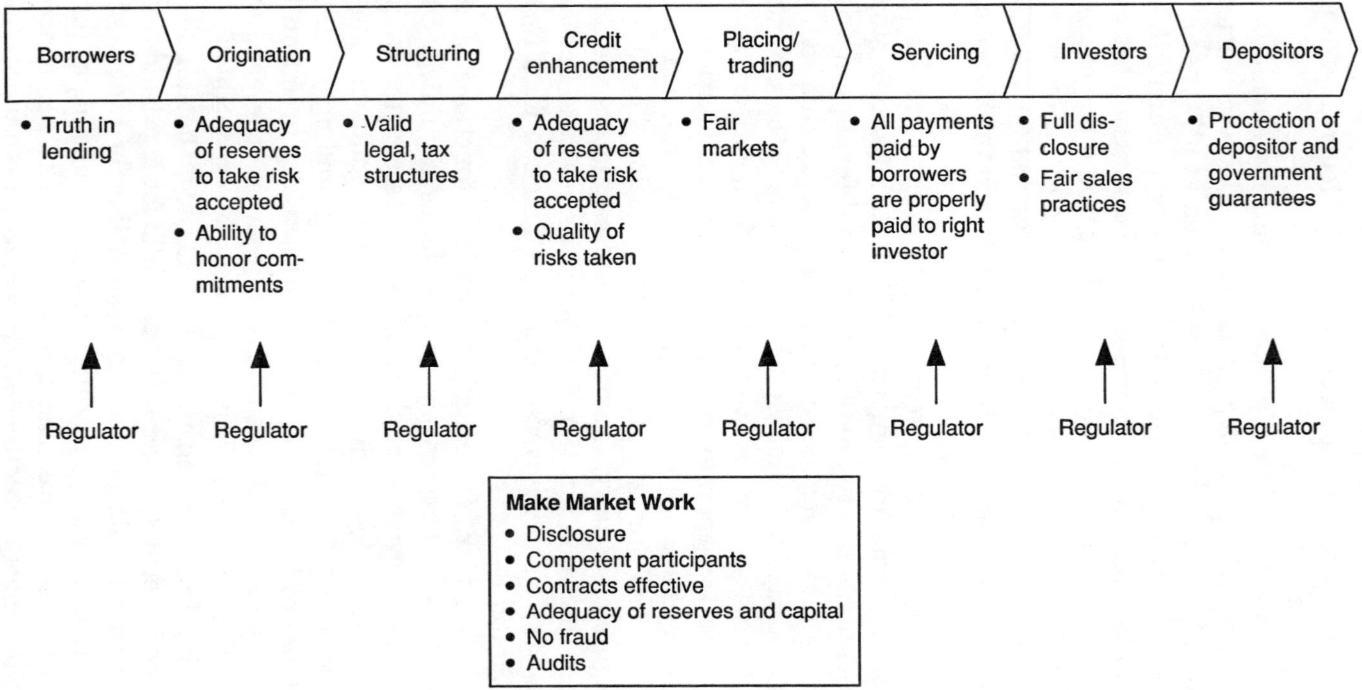

Borrowers	Origination	Structuring	Credit enhancement	Placing/ trading	Servicing	Investors	Depositors
• Truth in lending	• Adequacy of reserves to take risk accepted • Ability to honor commitments	• Valid legal, tax structures	• Adequacy of reserves to take risk accepted • Quality of risks taken	• Fair markets	• All payments paid by borrowers are properly paid to right investor	• Full disclosure • Fair sales practices	• Proctection of depositor and government guarantees
Regulator	Regulator	Regulator	Regulator	Regulator	Regulator	Regulator	Regulator

Make Market Work
- Disclosure
- Competent participants
- Contracts effective
- Adequacy of reserves and capital
- No fraud
- Audits

performed fairly and that investors benefit from full disclosure and fair sales practices. Another regulator could ensure that loan servicing is properly performed—so that, for example, all payments made by borrowers are paid to the right investors. Under this approach regulation would be tailored to the specific function and would, by definition, be consistent for everyone. Of course, the same regulatory body could regulate more than one of these specific functions as long as it was regulating each function for all players engaged in that function.

Many people reading this must be concerned at this point that I am proposing a large regulatory bureaucracy. Let me hasten to say that I am not. Rather, I believe the main function of these bodies should be to encourage private, market-based regulation. The burden of writing the rules should lie with independent, private, self-regulating enforcement bodies such as rating agencies and the Financial Accounting Standards Board. Private bodies, who rely on actual practitioners, are far better at writing rules for three reasons: first, because they understand the risks and best (and worst) practices more clearly; second, because they are more independent of politics; and, third, because they are more effective in adjusting the rules to changing conditions.

Because continued technological and financial changes are inevitable, we must build as much flexibility as possible into our regulatory system to keep it from becoming as obsolete as the system we have today. Under this scenario government regulators would be responsible for ensuring that these private bodies were effective, but the government role would be limited to oversight, rather than control or subsidy. Thus, for example, the government *would* get involved to ensure that risks and returns are transparent to investors through adequate accounting disclosure, that only competent participants are allowed to practice, that contracts are effective, that fraud is prevented, and that audits verify that assets, liabilities, and exposures are as stated. The government *would not*, however, provide a safety net function, except as needed for depositor and payment system protection.

3. *Regulate proactively.* As functional regulation is being written, our regulatory decision makers should work hard to foresee, and deal with, the problems that could arise from the new risks associated with our new financial technologies. Proactive regulation, at least in some areas, is possible if we work at it.

Moving to functional regulation gives us the opportunity to be proactive. The rewrite process should pull together the best practitioners in each phase of each new financial business system to define functional boundaries and to foresee and handle as many risks as possible, before they draw blood.

This is particularly important for securitized credit regulation and law. Securitized credit has developed within a legal and regulatory framework that was never intended to apply to this particular new technology. As a result, there are some unnecessary inefficiencies and some inequitable treatment of certain institutions. These inequities and inefficiencies will not prevent the development of the proposed new securitized financial system, but the system will be a better one after they are corrected. I suggest that a possible legislative agenda for a functionally regulated world might include at least several items.

First, reform is needed to assure consistent treatment of the first-loss credit guarantee by the originators of financial assets. Presently, finance companies can sell assets to a special purpose vehicle and provide limited recourse to cover expected losses on the assets. However, regulators currently do not permit commercial banks to effect sales of assets (for regulatory purposes) if there is any direct recourse back to the originating bank. Functional regulation would eliminate this disparate treatment and assure equal treatment of credit enhancement by all originators. Second, the bankruptcy code should be amended to provide, clearly, that financial assets transferred to a special purpose vehicle for securitization constitute a "true sale" of the assets. This "true sale" status is essential to protect investors from any bankruptcy proceedings against the originating institution. Presently, uncertainties in the interpretation of the bankruptcy code cause unnecessary expenses and complications in the structuring of securitized credit products. Similarly, the insolvency laws and regulations that presently apply to commercial banks create a small, unnecessary risk, in that an insolvency of an originating bank could cause the receiver to accelerate payments to the holders of securitized credit products originated by the bank. Investors dislike such call provisions; thus, this risk may create a further inefficiency. Of course, in a functionally regulated world both bank and nonbank originators would be subject to the same bankruptcy or insolvency standards.

Other possible legislative reforms might include the expansion of the REMIC (i.e., real estate mortgage investment conduit) tax classification to apply to other asset classes in structured securitized credit transactions. REMIC is a relatively new tax classification, created through an act of Congress, that allows mortgage assets to be efficiently securitized in "pay-through" structures that restructure the cash flows from the mortgages into tranches of mortgage-backed securities of different maturities. While nonmortgage assets can also be securitized through "pay-through" structures, these structures presently can impose some small additional costs because of some specially required, tax-related, structuring criteria. Another possible legislative reform would be to exempt special purpose vehicles from the Investment Company Act of 1940. The 1940 Act is mainly intended to protect investors in mutual funds and other investment companies. An unintended consequence of the 1940 Act causes it to prevent certain types of assets from being securitized through certain structures.

This legislative cleanup would make securitizing credit easier and would save legal expenses. The reforms are in effect artificial tariff barriers that slow down the speed with which technology evolves. A last possible legislative agenda item is to prohibit all institutions underwriting a securitized credit issue from selling it to either originator-sponsored trusts or to mutual funds for which the originator makes discretionary investment decisions. This reform would prevent structures from securitizing marginal assets and then placing the securities with investment pools under their control. Such placements may already be constrained or barred by the present law, but any such activity should clearly be declared illegal.

4. *Migrate risk away from protected institutions.* Assuming the clean up described earlier is underway, a critical step in building the new model would be to move to "risk-free" deposi-

tory institutions. Under this model federally insured depository institutions would only be allowed to invest deposits in short-term, or floating-rate, government bonds or securities (including nonfixed-rate mortgage-backed securities and other securitized loans) with credit ratings of AA or higher.

How can we convert today's banks and thrifts, which are anything but risk free, to this new environment? I would begin by unbundling them into functional subsidiaries and then taking action that would make it both expensive and administratively burdensome for risk-free depositories to make loans.

To a large extent, one tool that regulators are already employing—capital guidelines—could be used to motivate depository institutions to take risk-bearing assets off their balance sheets. Regulators could set capital guidelines for risks held by risk-free depository institutions that are clearly higher than the capital required to finance such risks outside the depository system. These guidelines would encourage the depositories to migrate all risk off their balance sheets either by placing them with commercial finance affiliates or by securitizing them.

For starters, capital guidelines like those now being introduced (as described in Chapter 5) could be ratcheted up year by year. These could be very effective, provided they are applied *only* to risk-free depositories (not to holding company affiliates) and provided that the regulators have the stop-lending and liquidation powers described earlier in this chapter. By requiring depositories to keep, say, 8 percent of loans in equity by 1992, 10 percent the following year, 12 percent the following year, and so forth, regulators would swiftly convince holding companies with depository institutions to take new loans off the depository institutions' balance sheet either by securitizing them or by placing them in a separate holding company subsidiary.

Further incentives for "risk-free" depositories to get rid of problem loans—indeed, all loans—could be provided by frequent rigorous audits using very conservative accounting standards (e.g., a mandated 50 percent loan loss reserve for any loan delinquent more than 60 days). Finally, compliance enforcement should include criminal penalties for those who grossly abuse regulatory rules, as some thrift executives and inside securities traders have already done.

Moreover, using a carrot, rather than a stick, could be effective. For example, "risk-free" depositories could be paid interest (perhaps equal to the Treasury bill rate) on their required reserves held with the Federal Reserve. Since under the new tax laws, profitable depositories will now have to pay full taxes anyway, the present system of not paying interest on required reserves in effect taxes profit making depositories twice: once through reserves and once through the IRS.

This kind of regulation would motivate any competent holding company to form two subsidiaries: a risk-free depository and a separate, credit-oriented subsidiary to take economic risks where the marketplace would provide the discipline against unwise risk taking. Obviously, to avoid the problems this system is designed to solve, the government would need to make it clear that it is *not* guaranteeing the liabilities of nondepository subsidiaries. Investors in these subsidiaries, and the holding company itself, would have to absorb any losses that resulted from bad risk taking.

Of course, moving to a "risk-free" depository system is not a simple task. One important complication is that it will take time to transform the current loan portfolios of most banks into securitizable loans that can be taken off the books. Good loans must become considerably more standardized than they are today, including provisions that allow them to be sold without the borrower's permission and that provide first-loss guarantees by the originator. Bad loans must be written off or worked out, or structured for sale, because the marketplace will not accept them in their current form. Moreover, it is obvious that banks will need time to create, staff, and properly capitalize nondepository subsidiaries into which they can move their loan portfolios. They will also need time to adjust their business system to the new environment. For all these reasons, existing loan portfolios will need some kind of "grandfathered" protection, and depository institutions will need the kind of slow, shaping regulatory process described above. While the average life of most bank portfolios is from 3 to 5 years, it will take at least a decade for these portfolios to turn over completely.

A second complication is that existing regulation and law actually discourages banks from cleaning up their balance sheets. Provisions of the Bank Holding Company Act of 1970 and the Investment Company Act of 1980 make it very difficult to remove bad assets from a bank balance sheet other than through the cumbersome "liquidating bank" structure which was used in the Continental Illinois restructuring by the FDIC and the acquisition of Texas Commerce by Chemical. These artificial barriers to getting bad assets off of bank balance sheets must be removed.

A third complication is that many small banks are not part of holding companies and some, in fact, are too small to justify setting up a holding company. If these institutions were to become "risk-free" depositories, they would have to get out of credit extension altogether because they would be unable to set up subsidiaries to hold the first-loss credit risk they need to absorb. Some would argue that these banks are too small to have sufficient credit skill to use depositor funds, but many successful home town bankers and thrift executives would disagree. Why should well-run small banks be punished for the sins of their poorly managed brethren?

A pragmatic answer to this issue might be to let all successful, well capitalized practitioners under a certain size operate as "grandfathered banks," as they have in the past, as long as they do not get into trouble. For example, any independent commercial bank or bank holding company with under $1 billion in assets that is complying with regulatory capital guidelines and that has a low percentage of criticized loans and charge-offs could be allowed to continue to operate as it always has unless (and until) it got into trouble—in which case it would lose its grandfathered status and would face stop-lending regulation or liquidation. Some 4,000 to 5,000 banks with some $200 billion in assets (i.e., about 8 percent of the industry's assets) would be in this group.

5. *Address payment system issues.* Finally, regulators should broaden their perspective to include the whole payment system, which includes much more than this country's regulated banks. The threat of "daisy chain" failure will not be entirely removed by the creation of a "risk-free" national depository system, although that will help. Here my answers are even less detailed than they have been up to now. My sense is that, conceptually, the longer-term answer is to move to a system of

simultaneous exchange of value, in which the trade of an instrument and the settlement of the transaction are simultaneous. That would eliminate counterparty risk. But we are a long way away from being able to move to such a system.

In the meantime, we need to find a method of protecting the payment system from default that does not involve, in effect, an unlimited guarantee by the federal government. There is no lack of will on the part of regulators to take on the payment system issues. The Federal Reserve System (and, in particular, the New York Federal Reserve Bank) is most concerned about the vulnerability of the payment system. However, the issue is caught up in the same legislative and regulatory gridlock that has blocked progress on all the other issues.

OUTSTANDING ISSUES

By this time, it should be clear to any reader that all I am doing is proposing a model and that much, much more thought is required. I am far from providing a detailed blueprint of the regulation that would be required to make this new financial system work.

I am more concerned about the broad legal and regulatory issues and the obstacles to overcoming them. Even with the best will in the world, the installation of a new financial system is a gargantuan task, requiring careful management and the involvement of hundreds of the best regulatory, legal, accounting, and practitioner minds. Unfortunately, I see little will to deal with the issues and some enormously difficult political obstacles.

CHAPTER 9

BENEFITS OF THE PROPOSED SYSTEM

In Chapter 6, I outlined the advantages of the securitized credit *technology* over the traditional lending practices of banks and thrifts today. Those advantages include better economics, better credit underwriting, better credit risk diversification, greater liquidity of assets, and the transfer of interest-rate risk to players better equipped to handle it than banks and thrifts are. The new *system* described in Chapter 7 would have all these advantages over the current financial system and many more. The unbundling of roles implicit in the new model and the shift to a risk-free depository system would yield even greater benefits to individual customers, to the banks and thrifts themselves, and to the public at large.

BENEFITS TO CUSTOMERS

All customers would benefit from products better tailored to their individual needs. Competition would be based on value added; as a result, each player would be working to understand the needs of its customers and to meet those needs at the best possible price. As noted earlier, there is no such thing as an average customer in financial services. For example, some customers prefer high service levels even if prices are high, while to others price is the most important buying factor. Some customers may want to see efficient handling of a high volume of transactions, while others may want customized handling of only one or two transactions a year. The financial service needs of bank customers are as diverse as the underlying economy.

If the business system is unbundled, it will be easier for each player to focus on providing tailored service to discrete sets of customers, rather than trying to serve the mythical average customer. Thus, for example, I would expect to see some players focusing exclusively on credit origination of particular asset classes—such as credit cards, mortgages, commercial loans, leasing, or commercial mortgages. Their product scope would be narrower, but most institutions would have a far wider geographic scope of operation than they do today.

Customers would benefit not only from tailored products but also from the greater availability of products that are relatively scarce today. As I noted in Chapter 6, securitization has already made long-term, fixed-rate mortgages available to many more consumers because it eliminates interest-rate risk for the lenders. As the system evolves, I would expect other customers—particularly small businesses and mid-sized companies—to also enjoy more long-term, fixed-rate credit availability.

On the other hand, it is true that borrowers who are not credit worthy may lose access to credit, since the securitized credit system contains controls that would put a stop to uneconomic lending (as described in Chapter 6). But frankly, given the misery caused by poor lending practices, I believe this tightening of credit standards will benefit many more people than it inconveniences. It may mean that people who want to raise quasi-equity money (for example, in leveraged-buyout finance) will have to pay more for their money, but that is as it should be. Why should individuals be massively enriched due to what is in effect a government subsidy?

BENEFITS TO BANKS

Despite the potential benefits, many bankers fear securitized credit because they believe it represents only a threat to them. Small banks, especially, see no role for themselves, except in mortgage origination; they expect that the larger banks and other nonbank players will use credit securitization to sap the remainder of their business away. It is true that almost no assets originated by community and local banks, except government-guaranteed mortgages, have been securitized up to now. And I must confess that I initially thought credit securitization represented an opportunity only for the major money centers and regional banks.

But, upon reflection and further research, I have come to the opposite conclusion. Ample evidence exists that small mortgage brokers and mortgage banks have been able to prosper in a securitized world. I now believe that credit securitization may represent one of the main ways that community and local banks can maintain their customer franchise and survive the tidal wave of change now transforming our financial system. The new technology would allow them to still originate many kinds of credit, and to diversify their credit risk through the trading of locally based assets for securitized assets originated in other locations, as described in Chapter 6. This trade would be accomplished through a conduit infrastructure, which would evolve naturally from the correspondent banking network that exists today. That is, regional and money center banks could provide the support needed to help small banks convert their loans into securities.

Looking past securitization technology to the proposed financial system as a whole, I see several, even greater, benefits for banks and thrifts that can rise to the challenge of adding value economically. The first, and most important, is that the system would create a multitude of new roles. These revolve around a new kind of specific, value-based competition that would replace the generalized, head-to-head competition that is such a no-win game today. The new roles would make some current barriers to competition irrelevant. For example, suppose a bank chose to focus on origination in one of its independent subsidiaries and chose to compete only in the few asset classes in which it had very good credit assessment skills. That bank would no longer be required to match off borrowers and depositors, limiting its lending according to its deposit levels (Exhibit 9-1). In fact, origination would largely be free from balance sheet constraints. In other words, a small player with superior origination skills would be able to increase its market share rapidly without having to raise a proportionate amount of deposits or equity capital.

EXHIBIT 9–1
Potential Future System

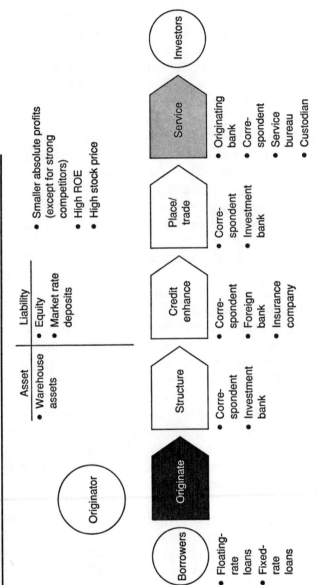

The system would create other roles for many banks. Structuring, the process of actually converting the loans into cash flows and repackaging them for investors, would become a major business, in which both investment banks and commercial banks (working with their correspondents) would compete. Credit enhancement, the process of underwriting and diversifying credit risk from investors would become a major business for publicly rated foreign banks as well as for insurance companies and the credit insurance subsidiaries of institutions that are today called bank holding companies.

Placing and trading the resulting securities would become an even bigger business than it is today as volumes continued to grow. These functions would probably continue to be dominated by investment banks, although (regulation permitting) there would probably be a major role for some affiliates of bank holding companies as well. Servicing the loans and the securities would also become an even bigger business, with the funds collection role continuing to be performed by the originating institution, and with the data processing and safekeeping roles being performed by a combination of commercial bank correspondents, service bureaus, and custodial banks.

In addition, there would be new roles related to deposit taking, which will now be legally separated from lending. Some institutions with strong franchises would be able to raise far more money from their depositors than they could place on their own risk-free balance sheets. The could serve these investors not only as a depository, but also (regulation permitting) by selling shares in money market mutual funds, bond mutual funds, and equity mutual funds that could be managed and serviced by nondepository affiliates (see Exhibit 9–2).

Further, the depository system would be unbundled along with the credit system. For example, I would expect to see the taking of deposits to be unbundled from the back-office processing of deposits through service bureaus. Most money market mutual funds already operate this way; the back offices of many market mutual funds are either the State Street Bank or the Bank of New York.

With such a wealth of roles to choose from, some of today's

EXHIBIT 9–2
Potential Future System, Depositors/Investors

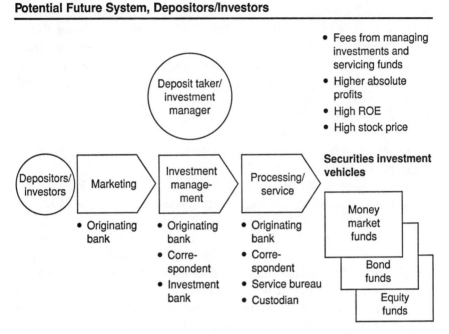

depository institutions would likely become very skilled at serving the needs of borrowers, some at serving depositors and investors. Others might continue to be strong at serving both borrowers and depositors; still others would carve out specialty roles by concentrating on one or two elements of the securitized credit or depository system.

Of course, once the field is staked out and specialized, and value-based competition begins among banks and nonbanks, winners and losers will emerge. Federal safety nets will no longer protect most businesses; finally, only the most prudent and most cost-effective specialized competitors will survive. The eventual number of institutions, and the roles they play, will be shaped by customers and economics, not regulation.

Under these circumstances the institutions successful at adding value in each business would enjoy far better performance than bundled banks do today, measured in terms of returns. In most cases, institutions that are commercial banks today would need fewer assets and fewer staff to perform the roles they have chosen. Banks that have chosen to concentrate on origination, for example, would have smaller balance sheets than they have today. They would need assets only for warehousing loans awaiting securitization and for liquid reserves to back up first-loss guarantees on the assets they originated. In many institutions the absolute level of profits would decline. But as the results of value-based competition played themselves out, we would begin to see an industry composed of far more effective institutions, earning far better returns on their shareholders' investment.

This performance would be recognized by stock analysts, who today are discounting many bank stocks. The discount stems from the fact that, for analysts today, banks are a "blind pool" of business risk. Analysts have no idea how much credit or interest-rate risk any single bank is exposed to—and when faced with the unknown, people generally assume the worst. Once the businesses in which the bank operates are separated into independent subsidiaries, the business risk will be far more transparent. Moreover, very soon each remaining business will be an efficient one, having sustained itself in a value-based competitive environment. I would expect the market value of institutions that emerge as capable players in some, or all, of their chosen businesses to rise.

Many bankers are uncomfortable with the prospect of needing less capital to do business; they wonder what to do with excess capital. However, successful players would have real opportunities to reinvest their capital in other business, and weak players, with low returns on capital today, would probably find the need for less capital a blessing, rather than a curse. Moreover, the large number of troubled, undercapitalized commercial banks and thrifts would be able to devote their skills to building business without the added burden of recapitalization. Frankly, I believe concerns of excess capital in the banking and thrift industries make little sense as credit losses continue to mount. I believe the concerns will shift to worries about how to be able to continue serving customers, and continue growing on the remaining capital base once the loan losses on existing portfolios have been absorbed.

Internally, these more value-oriented institutions would be far more manageable than today's banks. Businesses would be discrete: Business managers would serve a more homogeneous set of customers and oversee fewer activities with greater control over their costs and results. They could focus on real economics rather than deal, as they do today, with economics based upon judgementally based allocations of costs, capital, and revenue. Unwieldy, expensive, and often redundant corporate staff would be eliminated. Empires would be smaller, but they would run far more efficiently and effectively. Morale would no doubt improve; entrepreneurialism would be encouraged.

Strategically, banks that have been restructured into a series of self-contained, value-adding businesses should be far more comfortable about going forward in an ever more uncertain world, because their new structures will allow them to place multiple, independent bets on the future. At the outset, few institutions will have a clear idea of precisely where their competitive strengths lie—especially if, as is likely, restructuring takes place more or less simultaneously across the industry. But having restructured into a number of independent enterprises, each bank will be able to nurture those that are proving capable and cut off those that are struggling without suffering from excessive loss of blood. In contrast, those institutions that do not restructure could be dragged down completely because of problems in just one part of the business.

It is easy to see how this restructuring, and the subsequent pruning that would take place, would quickly solve the biggest problem of the banking and thrift industries today: overcapacity. No longer would the returns of capable institutions suffer from the existence of incompetent institutions that, propped up by federal safety nets, do uneconomic business for the sake of staying in business. Overcapacity would disappear both faster and more effectively this way than it would if banks stayed bundled and losers were simply allowed to fail, because the strong parts of each institution would remain in the system, while the uncompetitive parts either disappeared or were acquired by other institutions that could make more effective use of the capabilities.

BENEFITS TO THE PUBLIC

The public at large would benefit at least as much as the banks from the elimination of overcapacity and from improvements in efficiency and effectiveness. Today, the whole country suffers because of the low productivity of labor, funds, and capital in banking. And banks have a peculiar ability to transmit their overcapacity to other sectors of the economy. Overcapacity of lending has led to overcapacity in such sectors as agriculture or real estate construction. In Texas alone, for example, there are literally a hundred million square feet of unoccupied office space that would never have been constructed if local thrifts and banks had not felt compelled to lend. That was bad for the Texas economy, and the problem has had ripple effects.

Under the new system financial institutions would be stripped of any resources or funds that they could not productively use. Lending practices would be scrutinized by several disinterested parties before loans were securitized, and, therefore, only economic credit risks would be taken. In itself, this system of checks and balances would make credit extension more productive in real terms. In addition, the funds and capital released from depository institutions because they were no longer needed to support lending would find other, more productive uses. Funds and capital would continue to flow but through different channels. For example, as risk-free depositories paid below-market rates on deposits, depositors would reassess their need for government guarantees against higher returns from other nonguaranteed alternatives. Many would then move their deposits, for example, to money market mutual funds, which would in turn invest the funds in securities (including securitized credit). Thus, funds would flow in those channels that provided maximum benefits to funds providers and funds raisers, without government subsidy.

There would be other productivity benefits as well. By moving from thousands of full-service institutions to a smaller number of specialized providers, each operating with scale economies, our economy would reap the advantages of the factory over the job shop. Today, most small- and many mid-sized banks operate as job shops. In the future, each phase of the business system would be performed by the player of optimum scale. For example, while literally thousands of banks offer credit cards, the vast majority operate at a scale disadvantage. A small credit card issuer may have operating costs equal to 8 to 10 percent of loans outstanding. In contrast, a large player might operate at a cost of 3 to 4 percent of loans.

If all players operate with factory scale advantages, our economy would reap the maximum value for its resources. Further, the combination of scale advantages with the fact that the investors in securitized credit transactions demand lower returns on their investments than for less liquid lending business would generally reduce the total costs of the business that is now called lending. Specifically, the total costs of lending today—including capital costs, operating costs, and profit objectives—are about 4 percent of total loans, industry wide. A rough estimate is that the productivity savings available in the new system would eventually cut these costs by 1.5 to 2 percentage points or some 40 to 50 percent.

But finally, and most fundamentally, the proposed system would benefit the public because it would be sounder than the one we have now, without depending on artificial government subsidies of day-to-day business (which can encourage unsound lending) or massive government intervention in the event of credit default. As I have pointed out earlier, bad risk taking migrates in our current system. Not only can bad credit or treasury decisions destroy whole institutions; if those institutions are banks, their problems can be transmitted through the payment system to other banks. As I noted in Chapter 7, this is why the Federal Reserve has had to bail out such institutions as Continental Illinois or, more recently, First City Bancorporation (Houston). In contrast, risk in the proposed system would be contained.

Under securitized credit the special purpose vehicles used to do the deals would isolate the risks of each individual transaction from all other risks. Thus, even if a transaction were poorly underwritten, the resulting loss would not affect parties that did not participate in the transaction. In other words, while today it is the federal government that ultimately must absorb the risk of a disastrous credit decision by a depository institution, in the future the risk of a poorly underwritten securitized credit transaction would be borne by investors and credit enhancers. There would never be a need for a federal bailout—assuming that under the "risk-free" depository system, neither the end investors nor the credit enhancers in the transaction were federally insured depository institutions.

There may remain the need for a lender-of-last-resort function to prevent market panics, but this need already exists for major nondepository as well as depository institutions. If one of the major securities firms were threatened with failure, the Federal Reserve would surely step in to provide liquidity. But a lender-of-last-resort is not a guarantor; in providing the lender-of-last-resort function, the Federal Reserve should be able to avoid credit losses if it insists on adequate collateral before it extends emergency credit.

As a final point, let me describe why the proposed financial system would be sounder than our current system, by reflecting on how the Penn Square/Continental Illinois credit tragedy would have played out under the new rules.

First of all, it seems unlikely that the transactions would have ever been securitized. I doubt that any credit enhancer who did any homework at all would have been willing to guarantee the kinds of loans that were originated by Penn Square. I further doubt that the rating agencies would have been willing to rate the transactions, and without a rating the securities would have been difficult to sell to investors.

The second point is of course that Penn Square was a bank that took federally insured deposits. Under the system proposed, it would not have been permitted to take any first-loss risk. If it had been instead a pure loan originator, which was required by law to take first-loss risk, its ability to originate loans would have been limited because it had only $30 million in capital. If Penn Square had been required to keep a dollar of capital for each dollar of first-loss exposure, it would only have been able to originate $300 million of loans—even assuming that these risky loans only required a 10 percent first-loss guarantee to be securitized. If a Continental Illinois credit insurance subsidiary had provided credit enhancement, through a wraparound guarantee on the 10 percent first loss, it would have been exposed to at the worst a $30 million loss (assuming the Penn Square guarantee was completely valueless) rather than the multi-billion-dollar loss it wound up facing. Moreover, the sheer process of disclosure would have probably prevented the volume of loans to grow to that level. Even some of the top managers of Continental were apparently unaware of what was going on in Penn Square; if public disclosure had been made concurrently with the granting of the credit, as happens when loans are securitized, surely the unsound lending practices would have been ended sooner.

But assume for the moment that somehow $2 billion had been securitized and that a Continental Illinois subsidiary had guaranteed 10 percent of that amount and lost the entire $200 million. Under the proposed system the Continental Illinois depository would not have been affected, and there would have been no need for the FDIC or the Federal Reserve to intervene. The credit insurance subsidiary may have been forced into bankruptcy, but the depositors of Continental Illinois would not have been affected. Any losses beyond the credit of the credit insurance subsidiary would have been borne by the end investors, probably at least 100 of them. Even assuming a 30 percent additional credit default (i.e., a 40 percent total write-off), these investors would have, at the end of the day, suffered no more than a $6 million average loss (i.e., 30 percent of $2 billion divided by 100). In contrast, in the actual Penn Square/Continental Illinois transaction, the risk was concentrated in five banks, and all of them were significantly damaged.

Frankly, I believe that if legislators, regulators, and participants embrace the proposed system and take action to make it work effectively, we will wind up with a far healthier economy. Indeed, I believe the proposed new system could provide a key that helps unlock the current congressional and regulatory debate, which is caught up in issues of institutional self-interest versus the public good. And at the center of the debate are concerns about the soundness of the banking system, about the potential costs to taxpayers of the existing deposit insurance system, and about the absurdity of trying to keep securities and banking separate when the very process of credit securitization is making that separation impossible.

Do not get me wrong. I do not see this new system as a

panacea for all of the ills of the nation's financial institutions. It will not remove existing problem loans from the balance sheets of the nation's commercial banks and thrifts. Nor will it help out poorly managed commercial banks or thrifts that lack the skill to compete. But from the point of view of the overall economy, I believe this model deserves serious attention.

PART 3

TAKING ACTION

CHAPTER 10

THE WILL TO ACT

Up until now I have been describing the big picture: the system as a whole, the interests of the public at large, and the need for fundamental regulatory change. But the truth is that large-scale, nationwide changes are unlikely to happen soon. The task is too immense, and the sense of urgency is not yet strong enough to galvanize our lawmakers and regulators into action. In the meantime, the outlook of many banks and thrifts is becoming grim. What can these single institutions do to improve their situations while they wait for the regulatory relief that may be long indeed in coming? Luckily, there is a great deal to do. In fact, most of the actions that they should be taking now do not depend upon changes in either regulation or law.

I am now going to get personal. In the next four chapters I will address the managers of our nation's banks directly: Bank top managers, it is up to *you*.

The problem is that most bank top managers are unprepared to act right now. Most feel disoriented. The comfortable, traditional businesses you grew up with are becoming so fundamentally different that you hardly recognize them. Many of you have coped so far by denying that things have really changed and by acting as if somehow, miraculously, credit spreads will recover, competition will diminish, and new technologies will disappear. You behave as though what is going on is a cyclical trend rather than fundamental structural change.

But the transformation is real, and if you do not face up to that, your institution will fall victim to the overwhelming forces at work in the industry. If you want your institution to succeed going forward, you must begin by changing the way you view both your industry and your role. You must build the will to act in concert with the changes in the industry instead of resisting and denying that change is occurring. If institutions are managed aggressively to take on the challenges of the developing industry, they are likely to prosper. If not they will be victimized by events. If ever there was a top management challenge, this is it.

How should you go about developing the will to manage the institution through the unsettled times ahead? I believe you should move in stages. First, develop the courage to avoid taking either uneconomic credit risk or excessive interest-rate risk. Second, embrace the securitized credit technology rather than avoiding it. Third, decide to do the tough analytic work that will lay bare your institution's economics and its fundamental strengths and weaknesses. And, finally, build the courage to go your own way.

AVOID UNECONOMIC RISK

As pointed out in the first part of the book, many banks are taking the easy way out rather than facing up to the environment. They are preserving their net interest margins by taking excessive credit and interest-rate risk. In particular, they are taking credit risks where the net interest earned is less than their costs of capital and their expected loan losses. This is obviously a losing strategy.

If you do not want to be a loser, you must have the courage to resist business-as-usual pressures. This may mean abandoning lending where the risks now clearly exceed the returns. For example, for most banks the risks of lending to large corporations clearly exceed the returns; this is particularly true in leveraged-buyout and acquisition finance. The same can probably be said, for most banks, about the direct mail extension of credit through credit cards. Even in the middle corporate market, it makes no sense to lend money out at .5 percent over the cost of funds as some banks are now doing. One of the temptations that losing players succumb to is to make up for narrowed margins by adding volume. In trying to add volume all they do is add still more unproductive capacity, which exacerbates the overcapacity problem.

You must particularly resist the unsound, continuing erosion of lending standards and lending terms. It is bad enough to lend with low credit spreads coupled with low credit risk; this merely lowers returns on equity. It is worse to lend at nominally high spreads with high credit risk; this can destroy equity and, perhaps, your entire institution. The time has come to stop making loans where the risks and returns are unacceptable.

You need the same courage to avoid excessive interest-rate risk. At the same time that credit quality has been deteriorating, the globalization of financial markets has been creating market volatility unlike any we have seen in the postwar era. While so far that volatility has mainly been reflected in the foreign exchange, bond, and stock markets, no one should be lulled into thinking that short-term rates are here to stay. We have had three different periods of inverted yield curves from 1970 to the early 1980s, and in the process the thrift industry was so devastated that it has never recovered. Now not only many thrifts but also many commercial banks are making enormous interest rate bets and are thus fully exposed to a financial marketplace that continues to grow in power and turbulence.

As a top manager, your paramount concern must be to preserve the value of the institution you lead, in many cases, by making tough and unpopular decisions. I believe that if you can do it you will have enormous opportunities in a few years—at the expense of those who have given in to temptation and have been overcome by the turmoil.

EMBRACE THE NEW TECHNOLOGY

When faced with an overwhelming new technology, you can either become part of the technology or let it run you over. For the moment, it may seem easier to take excessive, but familiar, credit and interest-rate risks than to take on the changes and business risks represented by the new technology. But that will place you squarely in the path of the technology. If you want to move forward, I believe you must embrace the new technology, take up the tools it offers, and use them to define new, value-added roles for your bank (see Chapter 7, "Breaking Up the Bank"). In the last four chapters of the book, I will describe what some of these roles might be.

For most bankers, however, discussion of roles is premature. Relatively few have even begun to understand the securitized credit technology, its benefits, or its risks. We at McKinsey have found that one of the best ways to learn is to securitize some of your existing loans, because in the process you must come to grips with the technology.

To date, the institutions most willing to securitize loans have been those feeling the most regulatory pressure for more capital and paying the highest direct financing costs. Most of the better capitalized, more profitable players seem reluctant to consider using the technology for offensive purposes, although Morgan Guaranty and Citibank are notable exceptions. Most strong regional banks are still resisting the technology, and most community and local banks seem barely aware of what is going on.

Getting familiar with the technology is hard work, and it takes time. But it is worth the effort, because the technology is powerful and, as will be discussed in the remaining chapters, offers you a way to transform your institution's very role.

UNDERSTAND YOUR BUSINESS

In order even to contemplate breaking up your bank, you need first to understand where you add value and where you do not in your business.

This is easier said than done. As described in Part 1, bank economics are complex because the essence of the traditional bank model is a shared net interest margin, a shared cost base, and a shared capital pool. For example, few banks have accounting systems that can separate the net interest margin into its component parts (i.e., lending spreads, funding spreads, and interest-rate mismatching). Few banks understand the dynamics of their shared cost base. Many banks do not even allocate capital to risk-taking activities.

As a consequence, the top managers of even small banks, with relatively simple revenue and cost structures, often do not understand their fundamental economics. And the top managers of many larger banks face a hopelessly confusing set of numbers.

One tool we at McKinsey use to understand a bank's business economics is a *strategic cost/revenue diagnostic*. This approach avoids the difficulties associated with normal cost-allocation methods. It analyzes the businesses in terms of their unique and shared revenues and costs at each level of the current organization tree (Exhibits 10–1, 10–2, 10–3, 10–4). As part of this approach, net interest income is separated into income earned from lending, income earned from deposits, and income earned (or lost) from interest-rate betting (i.e. a matched-opportunity rate concept). Further, capital is allocated to each business. The objective of the diagnostic is to understand the costs and revenues of each business function.

While the process is conceptually straightforward, it takes massive energy to do it correctly. But it is worth the effort, however, because the final tree helps you identify where value is being added and where it is not. It also allows you to model dynamics (e.g., changes in volume, mix, pricing, costs) as well as the implications of taking different strategies.

In tandem with your cost revenue diagnostic, you need to carry out a skill assessment with a cold, analytic eye. Realistically, what is your bank good at? What is it not good at? How much of your profitability and cost structure is supported by adding real value to customers? There is no force imaginable, barring a devastating depression, that will put the genie of competition back into the bottle. As far as the eye can see, there will be more and more competition, as well as more and more value consciousness on the part of customers who will want to capture that value. The only safe harbor, long term, is to be able to deliver more value to customers than your competitors.

EXHIBIT 10–1
Cost/Revenue (ROS) Tree—Today

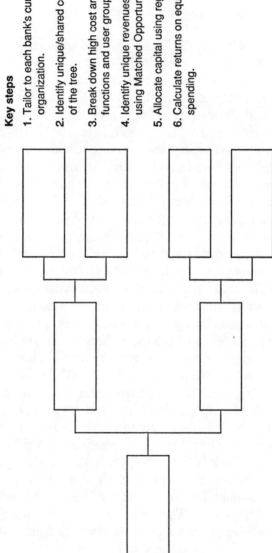

Key steps

1. Tailor to each bank's current organization.

2. Identify unique/shared costs at each level of the tree.

3. Break down high cost areas by major activities/functions and user groups.

4. Identify unique revenues at each level of tree using Matched Opportunity Rate (MOR) concept.

5. Allocate capital using regulatory guidelines.

6. Calculate returns on equity and returns on spending.

EXHIBIT 10–2
Identify Unique/Shared Costs at Each Level of the Tree—Start Top Down
($Millions)

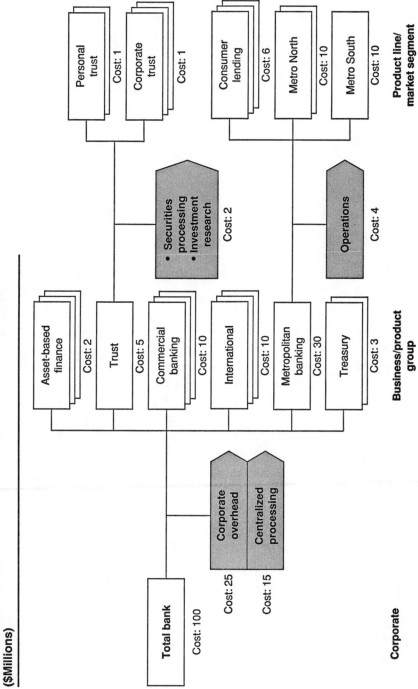

Product line/market segment

Personal trust	Cost: 1
Corporate trust	Cost: 1
Consumer lending	Cost: 6
Metro North	Cost: 10
Metro South	Cost: 10

Securities processing
• Investment research
Cost: 2

Operations
Cost: 4

Business/product group

Asset-based finance	Cost: 2
Trust	Cost: 5
Commercial banking	Cost: 10
International	Cost: 10
Metropolitan banking	Cost: 30
Treasury	Cost: 3

Corporate overhead
Cost: 25

Centralized processing
Cost: 15

Total bank
Cost: 100

Corporate

EXHIBIT 10–3
Break Down High-Cost Areas by Major Activities/Functions and User Groups
($Millions)

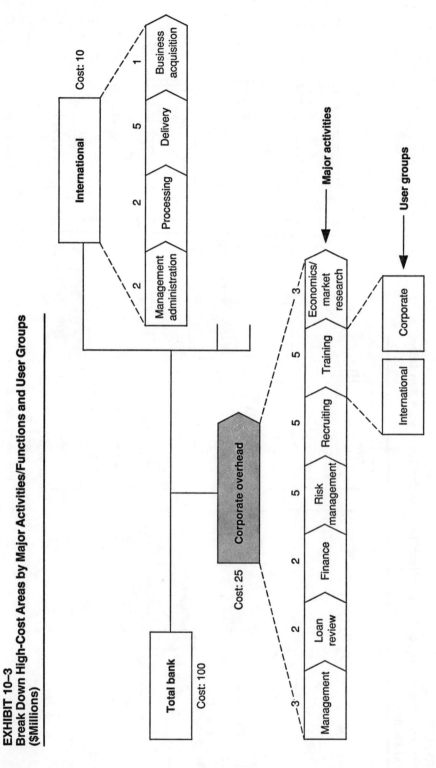

EXHIBIT 10–4
Identify Unique Revenues at Each Level of the Tree Using MOR Concept
($Millions)

- Start with existing transfer pricing
- Use matched opportunity rate to restate existing revenues
- Allocate equity capital using regulatory guidelines

Total bank

Cost:	100
Revenue:	130
Pretax profit:	30
Equity:	100

Corporate overhead — Cost: 25

Centralized processing — Cost: 15

Asset-based finance
Unique cost: 2
Revenue: 5
Equity: 5

Trust
Unique cost: 5
Revenue: 10
Equity: 5

Commercial banking
Unique cost: 10
Revenue: 45
Equity: 40

International
Unique cost: 10
Revenue: 10
Equity: 10

Metropolitan banking/branching banking
Cost: 30
Revenue: 30
Equity: 20

Treasury
Unique cost: 3
Revenue: 30 (Mismatch profit)
Equity: 20

145

And the truth is that many banks and thrifts are devoting too much of their cost base and their capital to activities where they add very little value.

GO YOUR OWN WAY

When an industry is awash with capacity, as the banking business is today, one of the worst mistakes you can make is to pursue the same strategy as your competitors. Historically, as described in Chapter 2, there has been little opportunity to pursue independent strategies, since regulation and oligopolistic pricing policies have limited your degrees of strategic freedom. Now, however, thanks to the breakdown of regulatory barriers and to the new securitized credit technology, there are a myriad of potentially new, value-added roles to choose from.

As I have just suggested, the role or roles you choose must be those in which your bank can add value. You will want to focus on those businesses, and functions within businesses, where you can have a cost or value advantage. The choices will differ from institution to institution, and yours will depend on your unique situation. In most cases, however, you should expect to redesign your bank completely—as Bankers Trust did in the early 1980s when it shed its retail activities. Let me say that another way because it is important: You should expect to reduce the size of your bank. In heavy competition the elimination of noncompetitive activities and functions is every bit as important as the buildup of competitive ones.

In this process it is essential to overcome the mind set that the institution has to be an integrated supplier. Banks have a tendency to do everything themselves, and the truth is that most of them perform many activities badly. For example, they tend to perform every function of the delivery of a product from product design, through marketing, selling, production, and after-sales service themselves, even though they could save enormously by subcontracting some of the functions.

It has always struck us, as we have worked with different institutions, how greatly they differ in effectiveness around different, discrete activities. For example, we have worked with two regional banks, of roughly the same size, to assess the effectiveness of their human resource functions. In one bank we found a human resource department that numbered 350 individuals accompanied by massive dissatisfaction throughout the bank about all kinds of personnel issues. In the other bank, the human resources function was composed of 15 individuals, and bank personnel were generally satisfied. The large department cost $20 million to run; the other cost only $3 million. The opportunity to restructure the larger department, and make it cost-effective, was enormous.

Once you develop the will to act, almost unbelievable transformations become possible. We saw one bank take a business with 5,000 employees that was losing $30 million a year and convert it, over just an 18-month period into a business with 2,000 employees earning $25 million a year.

Having completed your dispassionate self-diagnosis, many of you are likely to discover either that you lack the will to act, or that you lack the right management capabilities, or that you have limited competitive advantages on which to build. If so I would urge you to consider selling at the earliest opportunity while the value of your bank to an acquirer is highest.

Those of you who do have the management skill and the courage to act should move ahead quickly to develop an explicit plan for disaggregating costs and activities and restructuring them into cost-effective, value-adding business units over a period of time. Your bank will no longer be only one of thousands of similarly structured, full-service institutions; instead, it will be one of a smaller number of institutions, each with its own unique set of value-adding businesses.

In the next chapter, I will describe some of the roles that you should consider if you are heading a smaller institution, and I will outline some of the actions that assuming such roles would involve. In the final two chapters, I will make the same suggestions for larger institutions.

CHAPTER 11

CHARTING THE WAY:
SMALL INSTITUTIONS

One of the unique aspects of the U.S. financial system has been, and continues to be, the role played by small institutions. We have long been blessed with thousands of highly effective local and community bankers serving our enormously dispersed and varied economy. And there is no reason why many of these institutions should not be able to survive, and even prosper, in the new environment.

While many smaller institutions are severely troubled, many are not. Indeed, some are adding value now in unique ways that could become their cornerstones for success in a restructed financial services industry.

If you are the top manager of a small institution, one of the key issues you face is whether your bank, too, should be broken into component parts and reassembled. Many managers in that position will undoubtedly feel that the issues raised in this book are only for larger banks, but I would disagree. I believe that many small institutions will be far more valuable to their customers, and far better off, if they, too, adopt the model described in Chapter 7 and develop the will to act.

Perhaps not so incidentally, while this chapter is devoted to the issues facing small banks, much of it could apply equally to small, well-run thrifts.

THE SITUATION OF
SMALLER INSTITUTIONS

There are over 13,000 banks with less than $1 billion in assets. Eleven thousand of these are purely local banks with assets of under $100 million; most of these banks have only a single branch. The remaining 2,000 are community banks with assets of from $100 million to $1 billion; most of these banks have several branches that are usually clustered around one or two communities or a single city. Some of these banks are part of larger holding companies and, as such, are involved in the issues detailed in chapter 12 and 13.

The under $100 million local banks have, as a class, fared poorly during the 1980s. In 1986, excluding banks that were part of holding companies with over $1 billion of assets, they represented only 10.8 percent of the commercial banking industry's assets, down from 15.0 percent in 1981 (Exhibit 11–1). In general, they have been the most affected by the loss of the deposit subsidy, since many banks of this size had little lending skill and were primarily depositories. Many took on credit risk disproportionate to their size. As these banks lost deposit income and wrote off loans, their average after-tax return on assets fell from a very high 1.15 percent in 1981 to only .55 percent in 1986. Of course, it has hard to generalize about these banks as a class because the dispersion of performance has widened so dramatically, particularly because the returns of the worst banks have been devastated (Exhibit 11–2).

Many of the very smallest of these local banks are simply inefficiently sized. Without the deposit subsidy most banks with $25 million of assets or less are too small to be able to afford the trappings of being a bank: the board of directors, the regulatory reports, a president, and so forth. Moreover, the operating expenses of banks in this size range can be over 4 percent of assets, compared to operating expenses of roughly 2 percent of assets for an equivalently sized branch. As competition continues to make it more and more difficult for these tiny banks to earn a sufficient spread to keep in business, many are tak-

EXHIBIT 11–1
Local Bank* Share of Total Commercial Bank Assets (Percent)

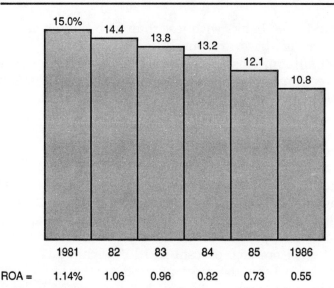

| ROA = | 1.14% | 1.06 | 0.96 | 0.82 | 0.73 | 0.55 |

*Banking organizations with under $100 million in assets.

Sources: FDIC; McKinsey analysis

ing lending or interest-rate risks they lack the skill to handle. Thus, both current economics and future risks argue for converting tiny banks into branches of larger community banks. This transformation would make them far more economic to shareholders and beneficial to the communities they serve.

On the other hand, relatively large single-branch banks, with over $100 million in deposits, can be very cost-effective. For example, a $100 million single-branch bank, with the same customer mix as the $25 million bank described earlier, may have operating expenses of only 2.5 percent of assets. These banks often exist in states such as Illinois or Texas that have a long history of unit banking laws (i.e., laws that prevent banks from having branches).

Community banks (i.e., multibranch banks with between $100 million and $1 billion in assets) have fared better than the smaller, purely local banks. Between 1979 and 1986 their share

EXHIBIT 11–2
ROE Distribution for Local Banks*

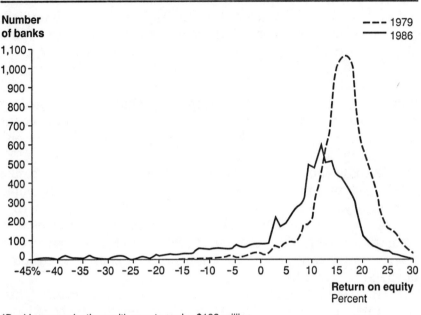

*Banking organizations with assets under $100 million.

Sources: FDIC; McKinsey analysis

of the industry's deposits declined only from 16 percent to 12.6 percent, while their mean return on assets fell only from .95 percent to .75 percent. Again, as with all other classes of banks, the dispersion of performance of community banks is enormous. For example, some of the better performing community banks have returns on equity of over 25 percent; some of the worst have returns of minus 45 percent.

UNIQUE VALUES TO BUILD UPON

Small, single-branch banks are relatively simple enterprises. Where these are successful, they are generally dominated by a single individual, usually the president, who is often also the principal stockholder. Whether the institution delivers value or not depends largely upon the skills of this single person. Many a small bank has floundered when its lead banker has died, retired, or changed jobs, because no successor with the same skills was available.

Community banks are relatively complex, as we at McKinsey have found in our diagnoses of a number of community bank subsidiaries of regional bank parent holding companies. Community banks usually have a management team of four or five key people, although there is usually one dominating personality.

The key competitive advantage of many community banks is often a reasonably dense branch structure in their home community. Whenever we do the work, we usually find that the banks with the largest share of well-located branches in a community (whether a community bank, a regional bank, or a money center bank) tend to get a disproportionately large share of the local deposits.

Many of these institutions are also successful lenders. They have substantial competitive advantages in many types of lending, because they know their local markets best. They have strong, trust-based relationships with the key decision makers in the community (local businessmen, real estate developers, lawyers, accountants, and the like), and they know how to convert these relationships into relatively high-yielding loans. The danger, of course, is that these loans are sometimes made without sufficient credit skill; when this has happened, community banks have gotten themselves into real trouble.

Some community banks also have surprising skill and cost-effectiveness in delivering particular, specialized services (such as trust services, commercial mortgages, residential mortgages). On the other hand, many try to offer a full range of services where they add too little value at too great a cost (for example, in credit card or indirect automobile loans).

It is thus very hard to generalize about small banks, as a class, since they are as diverse as the communities they serve— except for one thing. All successful smaller institutions do have one common characteristic: They all have a strong, local customer franchise. They know their local customers and their local market. If this local knowledge can be combined with cost-effective delivery and competitive products, then these institutions can compete with anyone.

BREAKING UP THE SMALLER INSTITUTION

Consider again the issue I posed at the beginning of this chapter: Are smaller institutions too small to disaggregate? The answer is: Not at all. In fact, I believe inefficiently sized local banks are too small to exist for long in today's competitive free-for-all *without* disaggregating. The key to longevity lies in developing the will to act and preparing for some very attractive, new disaggregated roles.

The essential disaggregation choices facing most local and community banks are whether to continue serving both borrowers and depositors, whether to focus on serving just borrowers as an originator, or whether to focus on just depositors as a "risk-free" depository.

Many local and community bank presidents will quickly say that they should continue to play both lending and depository roles, but they should avoid being too hasty. If you have a leadership position in such an institution, it is essential that you carefully analyze your competitive position first.

For example, if you are interested in an originating/loan service role, you need answers to questions such as: Which specific types of loans do we have a competitive advantage in originating (e.g., unsecured small business loans, equipment leases)? Can these loans be securitized? How fast? Will we still be able to maintain our competitive advantage if the loans are securitized? How much cost could be eliminated if we played only an originator role (and let others service and collect the loan)? Can we gain a sufficient volume of a particular class of loans to have bargaining power relative to a securitized credit conduit (you are almost certain to be too small to go to the market alone)? Can we really avoid the temptation to take excessive credit risk as margins get squeezed further?

If you are interested in a depository role, you need answers to questions such as: Do we have a sufficient density of well-located branches to remain competitive in our community? How much cost could we eliminate if we sold or eliminated all of our activities other than deposit taking (this assumes the deposits would be invested in largely risk-free assets)? Will other players be selling branches that we can use to build a more competitive, cost-effective branch network? Can we rent space in our branches to loan originators representing other institutions?

If you are interested in both roles, you need answers to the two toughest questions of all: Can we afford the investment required to be effective as both lending and deposit taking? Do we have sufficient management skill to be superior at both functions as competitive intensity continues to escalate?

I believe that the majority of the presidents of small banks, when they answer these questions honestly, will conclude that they face a far better chance of surviving and prospering by focusing on one role or the other, rather than trying to remain a full-service institution.

But this analysis leads to another question. Is not this advice to disaggregate a small bank simply theoretical? After all, many types of small bank loans, such as small business loans, have yet to be securitized. Moreover, there are as yet no securitized credit conduits that are focused on the small bank. So how could a small bank get its loans to the market?

In truth, the needed securitized credit infrastructure is not yet in place. And indeed, it will take several years before it is in place even with massive immediate investment.

However, this does not mean that you can not take action. For example, if I owned a small bank with a poor deposit base that was being subsidized by a strong lending franchise, what would I do? I would consider selling my bank—including the branches, the deposits, and the existing loan portfolio—to another bank and becoming instead a loan originator for one or more correspondent banks. In order words, I would originate loans for other banks to fund—including, most probably, the bank to which I sold my bank. But, instead of participating the loans as I always did before, I would use the capital I received in payment for my bank to guarantee the expected first loss on the entire portfolio. In return, I would expect a substantial share of the loan spread. The actual arrangements would depend upon the assets being originated. Having prepared to become a cost-competitive loan originator, I would next make a separate decision on whether or not to service the originated loans. The chances are that analysis would convince me not to, since most small banks are inefficiently sized servicers.

This kind of restructuring could greatly leverage the competitiveness of any small institution with good lending skills. For example, a small bank that has a clean loan portfolio, $50 million in deposits, and a $4 million net worth might be able to sell the assets and liabilities of the bank at a price equal to the net worth of the bank (i.e., $4 million) or more. That $4 million could provide sufficient first-loss guarantees for a substantial loan originating capacity. If we suppose that negotiations with the upstream correspondents wound up requiring a first-loss guarantee of 5 percent, then the restructured institution could originate some $80 million of loans—small business loans, consumer loans, residential mortgages, or whatever. The actual revenue split and first-loss guarantees between the originator and the correspondent bank would depend on negotiation.

If a significant number of small banks adopted this approach, they would hasten the development of a credit securitization infrastructure. If the purchasers of these loans were large, credit-worthy regional banks, these banks could pool the loans of small local originators together with similar loans from their own portfolios, reinsure the first-loss guarantee of the various originators, place the pool in a special vehicle, and securitize the pool. The correspondents would also be facilitating the progress of securitization by working closely with the various local originating banks to standardize terms, underwriting standards, and collection procedures.

Take a theoretical example of how such an approach could work with one of the most difficult types of loans to securitize: small business revolving credits. For this example let's also assume that regulators had blessed the structure. A regional bank could establish a standardized, but flexible, small business loan product (for example, a small line of credit priced at prime plus .5 percent with a $50,000 maximum credit limit and a 1 point annual fee to pay for the credit line availability). Each local originator would guarantee a 4 percent first loss on loan outstandings by its own borrowers and would back up this guarantee with an interest-bearing deposit in the regional bank. In this example assume that the originator kept the 1 point annual origination plus .5 percent of the loan outstanding. All of the loans from all originators (including the regional bank's own loans) would be put on the balance sheet of a commercial finance subsidiary of the regional bank, until the portfolio reached, say, $200 million (representing perhaps 1,000 loans). At that point some 75 percent of the portfolio would be of *randomly* selected and placed in a special purpose vehicle, while the other 25 percent was held in reserve to protect investors against prepayment. (Such an approach is already being used for credit card receivables.) Through a separate holding company subsidiary, the regional could guarantee a second loss of 2 percent around the securitized part of the portfolio, and a AAA credit enhancer could then surround the first- and second-loss guarantees with a wraparound guarantee of perhaps 10 percent. This would probably be sufficient to obtain a AAA credit rating for the deal. The loans would then be funded by commercial paper, and the spread between prime and the costs of the commercial paper would be retained by the regional bank as a servicing fee. The relationship with the borrower would be maintained by the originator, who would also be responsible for collecting the loans.

I will be the first to admit that this is a *theoretical* structure for these types of loans, but there is no reason why such a program (or a similar one) could not be developed for small business loans if the participants had the will to act. I will also admit that revolving credit small business loans may be one of the last types of loans actually securitized because of the difficulties in doing so, but that is why I used them in my theoretical example. Most of the other loans typically originated by local and community banks (credit card loans, automobile loans, commercial mortgages, and residential mortgages) have already proven to be securitizable.

So it seems to me that there is plenty of opportunity for those small banks that want to convert to a pure origination role. But what about the small bank in the opposite situation with a good depository base but an inadequate lending franchise or lending skills? If you are in this kind of institution, which is often a community bank with a strong deposit franchise, your lending operations are being subsidized by deposit taking. What can you do?

Again, if the decision were mine, I would first consider selling my loan portfolio and getting out of the loan originating and servicing business completely. Of course, this would not be easy; there are not many institutions interested in buying an entire small loan portfolio made up of a diverse variety of loans. But I could still go ahead and liquidate my loan portfolio, by putting up for bid to other lenders those high-quality loans in my portfolio with relatively standardized servicing requirements (such as residential mortgages, credit card loans, commercial mortgages). Depending on their rates, credit quality, terms, and ease of converting to another servicer, these loans could be sold at either a premium or discount from face value. The less standardized loans would simply have to be collected; my guess is once an announcement had been made, most creditworthy borrowers would change banks voluntarily. This would leave a residual core of problem loans that would simply have to be worked off.

I would also want to consider a different, possibly much better option: that of affiliating with an institution that had strong lending skills (probably a correspondent bank) and that could take over the management of my entire loan portfolio. Under this option the potential affiliate would thoroughly review my entire portfolio, work through what it would take to convert the existing loans to its own systems, and make a bid. In looking for a potential partner I would bear in mind that experience in conversion is valuable and—for the time being—rare. Therefore, I would seek a bank that has already come part of the way down the learning curve by previously acquiring other institutions. In the selling process I would negotiate with institutions on such features as first-loss guarantees on the sold loan portfolio, price, and servicing and collection responsibilities. The affiliation agreement might also include a provision that enabled me to continue to originate loans using space rented in the branch. Once my loans had been completely sold off, I would simply take the proceeds and invest them in high-quality assets, while eliminating all of my lending activities (i.e., creating a "risk-free" bank). A variation of this approach would be to get out of most lending activities completely but continue to serve as an originator for one or two particular types of loans where my institution possessed real lending skill.

TAKING ACTION

If you have developed the will to act, as described in the last chapter, and if one or more of the roles I have already described appeals to you, your next step should be to get answers to the kinds of questions I have suggested above. Your goal will be to determine in which role your bank will deliver the most value to your customers. Your choice should reflect your assessment of your bank's own skill base, the skills of your competitors, your current economics, and your possibilities for negotiation with others. You may decide it makes more sense to sell your whole enterprise and let the buying institution deal with the restructuring issues.

To the extent that economics drive roles, I would expect most people who run small, single-branch, local banks to sell to community or regional banks and transform their banks into branches. Having done that, they could proceed to play an origination role within that branch, operating much as small local insurance brokers or mortgage brokers operate today. I would expect most people who run community banks with strong branch systems to continue to concentrate on deposit taking, with many playing strong origination roles as well, albeit with a narrower range of loan products. While these would be common patterns, many small bankers would probably find opportunities to build upon unique skills as the basis for specialized, innovative roles. For example, some community bankers with strong trust strategies might specialize in retail securities brokerage or in selling and managing money market, bond, and equity mutual funds.

Because the decision on roles is so important, you must make every effort to make the best possible decision, and that means gathering information. While some of the information you need is internal, such as the results of the strategic cost/revenue diagnostic described in the last chapter, much of it is external. You need the viewpoints of customers and board members to help develop an objective picture of where your bank is truly adding value, and of what your competitive strengths and weaknesses are. You need substantial discussion with the correspondent banks who are your potential affiliates to understand what your options are for participating in various kinds of networks. And you should participate whenever you can in forums and conferences sponsored by your trade associations such as the Robert Morris Associates, the American Bankers' Association, and the Bank Administration Institute, to gain a better understanding of the trends transforming the industry and to discuss these issues with your peers. Importantly, your small size gives you the freedom to discuss potential roles and strategies with other top managers of small banks. Because as small banks your geographic scope is limited, you are far less likely to find yourselves in direct competition than the heads of money center or large regional banks would be.

Your small size gives you another advantage during this time of transition: Whatever role you choose, whichever approach to restructuring you take, the transition will be manageable. Unlike the money centers and major regionals, you can expect to implement virtually any of your restructuring options within a year or less. Therefore, while you should certainly develop your *plan* for restructuring as soon as possible, you can set the timing of your move to match your individual bank's circumstances.

In general, I would advise waiting as long as waiting does not diminish the value of your institution. That is, if your bank is suffering today, your strategic options are likely to be limited to selling—and since your value will probably never be higher than it is now, it makes sense to sell now. On the other hand, if your institution is thriving, it makes sense to continue to build your financial strength while you wait for greater regulatory clarity and further developments in the marketplace. With more certain knowledge, your restructuring will involve less risk.

Regulatory clarity is likely to be a long time coming. As I have already noted, we do not know when the breakdown in the credit system will reach crisis proportions, or what the impact on individual players and industry economics will be, or what changes in regulation and law will result. As a class, small institutions potentially have enormous clout with legislators on regulatory issues if they can present a unified front. If, for example, small institutions were to support the kind of regulatory changes described in Chapter 8, then the likelihood of their becoming a reality would be significantly greater. Realistically, however, it seems unlikely that we will see regulatory clarity earlier than 1990, since a complete legislative and regulatory overhaul is highly improbable in the first year of a new president's administration.

Developments in the marketplace may come faster, especially if small institutions encourage them. For example, consider the infrastructure that will give small institutions access to the securitized credit technology. If small institutions want support, and negotiate for it as I have suggested, the development of the infrastructure will be rapid. Otherwise, it will be slow.

Whether you are a potential buyer or seller, there is one action you should begin now: Start investing behind those activities where your institution adds real value to customers and begin to eliminate activities where it does not. Under almost any circumstances, focusing and finding means to add real value to local customers will pay off for the smaller institution.

CHAPTER 12

THE VALUE OF BREAKING UP THE LARGER INSTITUTIONS

The overwhelming bulk of the U.S. banking industries activities, and roughly 78 percent of its assets, are now concentrated in some 260 large bank holding companies, which contain over 2,200 banks (Exhibit 12–1). It is these large, complex organizations that have the most to gain from being broken apart and reassembled into more valuable institutions. Top managers in these institutions face both huge opportunities and tremendous challenges.

Of these 260 large banking institutions, each of which has over $1 billion in assets, we have, for the purpose of this book, classified 250 as regional banks and 10 as money center banks. While one can argue over terminology, we have labeled banks as money center banks if they have historically been referred to as money centers and if they remain committed to the national large-corporate market and to international banking. However, as the forces described throughout this book have caused the industry to diverge more and more, it has become increasingly difficult to generalize about any of these institutions.

On the other hand, it is possible to make a few observations about some broad trends. For example, it is easy to see that there has been a massive transfer of relative importance from the money centers to the regional banks during the 1980s. Regional bank holding companies now account for over 53 percent of the nation's banking assets compared to 45 percent in

EXHIBIT 12–1
Commercial Bank Assets, 1986 ($Trillion)

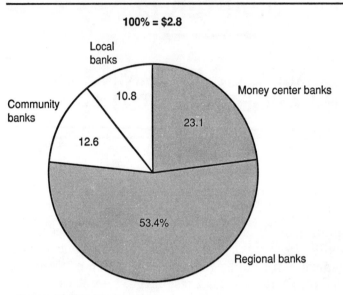

100% = $2.8

Local banks

Community banks

10.8

Money center banks

23.1

12.6

53.4%

Regional banks

Sources: FDIC; McKinsey analysis

1981. In comparison, the share of assets held by the 10 money center banks actually fell from 25 percent to 23 percent over the same time period (Exhibit 12–2).

Some money center banks that have visible troubles are already talking about restructuring. On the other hand, regional institutions, particularly those performing well, would probably wonder why they should even consider taking such radical action. The answer, I believe, is twofold: first, most large bank holding companies could benefit greatly from breaking the banks in it apart and reassembling the parts; second, the trends I have seen in regional banking suggest to me that sooner or later the regionals too will come under pressure to be more cost-effective competitors, and they will find that restructuring is their only feasible option.

But before considering how restructuring can benefit your large bank holding company, let us first explore the situation facing regional and money center banks today.

EXHIBIT 12–2
Money Center and Regional Bank Share of Commercial Bank Assets
(Percent)

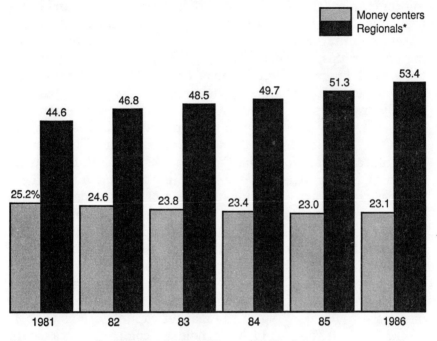

*Nonmoney center banking organizations with over $1 billion in assets.

Sources: FDIC; McKinsey analysis

THE SITUATION OF REGIONALS

As with other classes of banks, the dispersion of performance among regionals is enormous. For example, in 1986 the best performing regionals (i.e., the best 25 out of the 250) had an average return on equity of about 22 percent, while the worst performing regionals (i.e., the worst 25 out of 250) had an average return on equity of minus 10 percent. Much of the performance differential was due to the underlying health of the regions in which they operated. For example, New England regionals all tended to be strong performers during the 1980s, and Texas regionals all tended to be poor performers.

However, much of the differential in performance has also been due to relative size and skill. The regionals themselves are divided between dominant or *super* regional holding companies (these have over $15 billion in assets) and other regionals. I believe that it is only a matter of time until most of these remaining regional banks consolidate into 50 to 80 *super regional* groups, because of the significant competitive advantages that bigger regionals enjoy over smaller regionals and many other smaller banks in their regions.

By any measure, the super regionals have been performing very well. They include such institutions as Barnett Banks, BancOne, Bank of Boston, Bank of New England, First Union, Core States, First Wachovia, Fleet-Norwest, NCNB, Pittsburgh National, SunTrust, and Wells Fargo just to name a few. These super regionals are exceptions to many of the trends described in the first part of this book. They have grown in both size and profitability, and they have kept credit losses at minimal levels. In fact, many have had the profit strength to write off or sell off most of their loans to developing countries at the same time that LDC debt has been severely damaging many of the money center banks. Their relative success can easily be demonstrated by looking at the market capitalizations of their stock. In 1980 the list of bank holding company stocks with the highest market capital or actions was dominated by money center banks; today the list is dominated by super regionals. For example, in March of 1988, seven of the 10 bank holding companies with the highest market capitalizations were super regionals, with only Citicorp, J.P. Morgan, and Bankers Trust remaining in the top 10.

The super regionals have succeeded by using the traditional bank model but making it work far better than their competitors have done. Most of these holding companies have at their core one or more large banks. These banks typically have a dominant position in at least one important regional city (such as Atlanta, Boston, Charlotte, Columbus, Philadelphia, or Pittsburgh) and possess dominant market shares of deposits in those cities (i.e., 25 percent or more). Entering the 1980s these banks had developed a broad range of services for the individual correspondent bank and corporate marketplaces. In particular, they had enormous strength in operations and systems due to their role in regional check clearing. As geographical barriers to interstate regulation fell (through regional compacts), these banks had the skills and scale to offer more value to customers than smaller regional and local banks. They could offer a broader range of more sophisticated products, because their larger customer base justified more product development. For example, they could offer their middle market customers interest-rate swaps and corporate finance services. They could use their credit skills, which are often superior to those of the smaller regionals with which they compete, to ensure a healthy loan portfolio. And they could use their organizational skills to achieve economies. During the 1980s many of these super regional bank holding companies discovered that they could acquire smaller banks, even at hefty premiums, and more than pay for the acquisition by eliminating redundant costs and increasing prices. In particular, they discovered they could eliminate the smaller bank's overhead function and then use their operating and systems skill to consolidate the smaller bank's operating costs with their own and use their pricing skills to increase prices for selective services up to the price levels they were already charging for similar services in their home market. In other words, they acquired distribution and customers, raised revenue through repricing, and saved costs through eliminating redundant capacity.

While it is hard to quantify revenues raised through repricing, cost savings can be estimated. For example, consider what NCNB has accomplished: NCNB acquired eight banks between 1982 and 1985. These banks had assets of $6.4 billion, and before acquisition their ratios of operating costs to assets averaged about 350 basis points. Before the acquisitions began the same ratio at NCNB was 260 basis points. Today, it is 270 basis points. We at McKinsey estimate that the efficiencies NCNB has achieved have added about $18 million to the bottom line of the acquired banks (this was 9 percent of NCNB's 1985 income before taxes). Moreover, some of the acquisitions are recent. Since it takes time to wring out inefficiencies, we suspect that NCNB is not finished saving yet.

This experience appears to be relatively common. McKinsey analysis has shown that a large regional bank can usually operate at significantly lower costs than a smaller regional with the same customer mix and the same basic product line. For example, a $15 billion regional bank might have operating costs of 2.5 to 3 percent of assets, while a $3 to $4 billion regional bank might have operating costs of 3.5 to 4 percent of assets.

In summary, these regional bank holding companies have succeeded at old-fashioned banking. They have been cross-subsidizing products and customer groups like everyone else, but they have been operating at lower costs and offering their customers better value than most of the smaller regional and community banks with which they compete. As a result, their net interest margins and fee incomes have grown faster than their shared costs, and they have been profitable enough to resist the temptation to take excessive credit or interest risk.

Thus, in comparison to all other sectors of the banking system, many of the super regionals are in excellent shape. They have relatively strong customer franchises and relatively strong management skills, and they are relatively cost-effective. This combination has enabled them to enjoy fundamentally strong profits and to maintain fundamentally strong balance sheets, while much of the industry is weak. Their stocks trade at a premium to book at a time when most of the industry trades at a discount, and they can use that stock value to continue to acquire other banks. They have enormous opportunities to win.

They can not afford to be complacent, however, because their current competitive advantages are temporary. The success of the super regionals has been based on their ability to grow, to achieve some scale economies, and to outperform their smaller competitors. But in some regions the limits to growth are looming. In the Northeast and Southeast regional compacts have been allowed by regulation since the early 1980s; the super regionals there have only a few moves left. In the Midwest the consolidation process has only recently been approved by state legislators; this and the recovery of the economy of the manufacturing Midwest suggest bright prospects for the budding super regionals in that area over the next few years.

At some point, however, the consolidation opportunities will be exhausted. My guess is that in three to five years the regional consolidation process will be complete. At that time, the super regionals will no longer be able to succeed by out-performing smaller institutions; they will instead be competing against each other and against successful national players—including American Express, GECC, and Sears, as well as Citicorp. They will no longer enjoy value or cost advantages, and they will have to compete based on price. (This is already happening in some key regional product markets; for example, credit margins in middle-market corporate banking are beginning to resemble those in the large corporate market.)

As price competition increases and margins come under pressure, some super regionals will inevitably be tempted to keep their net interest margin up by taking excessive credit or interest-rate risk. Having done that, they will become vulnerable to recession— which must come sooner or later—and the same pattern affecting the rest of the industry can affect institutions now regarded as pillars of strength. Indeed, regionals are vulnerable to credit risk. For example, Mellon has already been hurt badly because it focused on short-term profits and stock price growth and accepted greater credit risk to mask developing earnings weakness; in this case top management was replaced. At First City Bancorporation (Houston) and First Republic Bancorporation (Dallas) the problems of excessive risk taking have been far more devastating.

I have said the excessive risk taking by some players seems inevitable; so it is, unless regulation is changed along the lines I have suggested in Chapter 8. By mandating a "risk-free" depository system and forcing institutions to fund lending with market-controlled resources, our nation's regulators could in effect protect our super regionals (and other banks as well) from themselves. If I were the top manager of a super regional, I would not depend on that. I would work, now, to protect myself.

THE SITUATION OF MONEY CENTERS

In comparison to the regionals, the money center bank holding companies have lost both relative power and profitability. They are still enormous institutions; just the 10 we define as money center (e.g., Bankers Trust, Chase, Chemical, Citicorp, Continental Illinois, First Chicago, Irving, J.P. Morgan, Manufacturers Hanover, Security Pacific) account for $700 billion in banking assets. (We have excluded Bank of America from this list because that institution has recently been restructured to look more like a regional.) Unfortunately, the money centers are saddled with loans to developing countries, which are for this group a bigger credit problem than domestic debt. In the first three quarters of 1987 these institutions collectively lost over $5 billion, primarily because of LDC debt provisioning. Many analysts question whether these provisions are large enough yet. And some analysts wonder whether the financials of some money center banks contain other, hidden time bombs—such as large blocks of leveraged-buyout or acquisition finance.

The problems of money center bank holding companies are compounded by the enormous decline in the profitability of their large corporate customer base, which I have already described. It is hard to overestimate the impact of this loss. Money center banks, as we know them, were created largely through mergers in the 1950s and 1960s, primarily to serve large corporations better. They went international as their customers became multinational. As the credit spreads on lending to large corporations have evaporated worldwide, and as securitization has advanced, many of these banks have been left with an infrastructure designed to serve a customer base that will no longer pay for it. While this customer base still represents enormous opportunities for some, notably in operating services and corporate finance, those opportunities are only available to institutions with truly distinctive capabilities.

Despite their all too visible problems, many of the money centers clearly have enormous strengths. A number of them contain powerful regional organizations. Some, such as Citicorp, Chase, and First Chicago, have become powerful national competitors in credit cards. Others, such as J.P. Morgan and Bankers Trust, have developed merchant banking and trading capabilities on a par with the leading investment banks. In fact, even more than other types of banks, money center banks are becoming so diverse that it is increasingly difficult to describe them as a class. Of the 10, only Citicorp still seems to wish to serve all classes of customers, with all types of products, worldwide.

But while only Citicorp apparently still has the ambition to be an across-the-board competitor, most of the other money center bank holding companies still find themselves with huge investments in business and in geographic locations where they enjoy no competitive advantages. As competition has eroded their profitability, and as their ability to cross-subsidize weak businesses with the profits from strong businesses has disappeared, their managers have been looking harder at their cost structures. Some have found huge chunks of dedicated cost that are relatively easy to prune away, with no loss of effectiveness and that might have been shed much earlier. But most of these holding companies are also burdened by *shared* infrastructure costs designed for an era long gone. This restructuring will be hard, but it is essential if the money centers are going to survive in the value-based competitive environment of the future.

THE MANAGEMENT CHALLENGE

Even though regional and money center bank holding companies are performing very differently today, I am struck by the similarity of the challenge that faces all who lead these institutions: Essentially, it is the challenge to make the institutions manageable and competitive. The two really go hand in hand; today large bank holding companies are uncompetitive, or becoming that way, largely because they are, or are becoming, unmanageable. Let me explain what I mean.

Money center banks began to face a set of interrelated economic and organizational issues a few years ago; super regionals are starting to face the same set of issues now; regionals in the first stages of consolidation will face them very soon. Margins are (or will be) under pressure. The business is becoming increasingly complex. Costs are rising to the point to where bankers are finding it more and more difficult to afford all the investments they feel they should be making (a difference here is that money center banks have invested both internationally and domestically, while regional banks have invested to broaden their domestic operations). And finally, whether the scope of the business is domestic or international, bankers are finding their management structure overwhelmed by the sheer volume of important business decisions that must be made. Without real management, businesses can become mediocre, or worse.

A shared cost structure places most of the management burden at the upper levels of management where the information needed to make decisions and the power to enforce them is located. Top managers today are required to make so many decisions, across so many geographies, so many functions, and so many businesses that they worry about having the time to make them all wisely. Faced with the enormity of the job, some simply try to work harder and harder—and still find that there are not enough hours in the week to do everything that needs to be done. Others look for ways to make the job simpler.

One way of simplifying is to retreat into something familiar, such as controlling risk, or putting pressure on subordinates to meet budget, or cutting costs. The problem with this solution is that the people under the chief executive who receive these directives generally lack the information, the skill, and the general management perspective needed to make high-quality decisions. The wrong costs get cut; the wrong steps are taken to meet budget.

Another way of simplifying is to deny the need for change; this is probably most attractive to leaders of successful super regionals. The classic response is: If the bank is not broken, there is no need to fix it. I have heard this point of view from many bankers in the past. More often than not, I have watched the businesses run by these managers suffer over time. Eventually, businesses that do not respond to change weaken.

The management challenge for you as a bank leader then is to transform your bank's management and cost structure so as to create management jobs that can be performed by real people, not super humans. Your institution's chances of success, and its value to shareholders, will increase dramatically if it is populated by dozens of highly capable individuals, with manageable jobs, each making relatively few decisions with sufficient information, time, and power to get them right. That is, your people must be able to make the businesses they run capable of competing cost-effectively on a value-added basis.

Individual managers will, of course, approach this transformation with a different goal in mind, depending on their bank's current financial condition. If it is troubled, the goal will probably be to maximize the value of the institution, or parts of it, to one or more potential acquirors. If it is healthy, the goal will probably be to strengthen it to compete in the environment I have already described.

Whatever your particular circumstances, I would urge you to act promptly. You may not feel a sense of urgency (for instance, if you are heading a successful super regional), but it makes no sense for even a winning bank to continue to cross-subsidize losing businesses, or spend money unproductively, just because it can afford to. Nor does it make any sense to sub-optimize opportunities, or take unnecessary risk, or watch competitors take over your franchise, simply because your organization lacks the capacity to manage. I would advise you to attack the task now, while your strong financial position gives you the resources to form a number of attractive business units and staff them with the best management talent in the industry. Your strength gives you room to maneuver, and time to act. Do not squander it.

BREAKING UP THE BANK

By this time, it will not surprise you that I believe the best way to make the management job doable and the bank competitive on a value-added basis is to break up the bank. By doing this you will be able to address your margin problems very effectively—not by cutting a little here and a little there, but by designing the system you need to win and then eliminating everything else. When you do the right analysis you will find that an awful lot of activity (and the related expense) is completely unnecessary. Too much management energy and too much spending are devoted to businesses in which the institution lacks any real strength. If you get out of these and redesign what is left around a smaller number of activities, you will likely have the resources to do at least some of those that remain very well. One advantage big banks have is that they are in nearly everything now and have a lot of skills and capabilities that would be very valuable if they were focused properly. Of course, you must act with caution. Many institutions have cut costs only to discover that they just got out of something that they really needed.

What exactly do I mean by "breaking up the bank" for a large institution? Essentially, I mean that you should be looking to convert your large, integrated bank holding company into a number of more decentralized, more self-contained businesses. First of all, this would involve creating a number of true general management points below the chief executive, in some cases two or three levels below. Each general manager must have real autonomy to act and support functions dedicated to his or her business. Achieving this will usually mean restructuring the centralized corporate staff and decentralizing all but a few essential corporate staff activities under the decentralized managers. In addition, you may want to restructure individual banks, as was described in Chapters 7 and 11, so that lending is separated from deposit taking.

All of this is, of course, easier said than done. You must accomplish the transition while still protecting your institution from credit and other risk and while maintaining its overall cost-effectiveness and profitability. But the rewards of successful restructuring could be very high. At the end of the day, your restructured institution will be more manageable, more competitive, more flexible, and more valuable to investors.

More Manageable

By creating a number of general management points, you will give more of your people the room to grow leadership skills and thus gain the support of a whole cadre of leaders rather than just a handful. These leaders will be effective, because your restructuring will create positions that can be held accountable for results. By creating self-contained businesses you will eliminate the ability to cross-subsidize failure or to succeed by winning mere management information system arguments (such as getting the lion's share of credit for revenues shared by multiple businesses, getting someone else to bear most of the cost allocation burden, or getting someone else to bear the costs of capital).

When you self-contain a business, the manager in charge can not hide. His or her results can be truly compared to independent, competitive companies in the same line of business.

In my work with some of the better nonbank financial companies, I often see the benefit of such clear autonomy. The transparency of results focuses the mind terribly. All of a sudden there is an accountable point for decisions. No one is confused about who is responsible if there are cost overruns, or if bad credit risk is taken, or if there is a revenue shortfall, or if there is an inadequate response to competitive or technological change.

Self-containment takes the sloppiness out of decision making. Decisions are no longer made by committees where no one is really in charge. Decisions are no longer avoided because problems slip between the cracks. Accountability is clear.

More Competitive

Through self-containment the business system can be better tailored to the critical success factors of the particular business. The critical success factors differ widely between, for example, the credit card business, branch-based deposit taking, corporate finance, and wholesale operating services (e.g., cash management). The very management culture, "the way we do business around here," needs to be different. Too often, however, banks try to manage diverse businesses like these as if they were all the same—which is not surprising, since they tend to be overseen by the same general manager or same staff functions.

People tend to manage based upon what they know. If you make a banker with a corporate marketing orientation the general manager of a geographic region, he will tend to treat it as if it were a wholesale business. The same is true in reverse; I have watched many retail managers placed in geographic management positions subconsciously wind up concentrating exclusively on retail branch banking and other businesses they know.

By more sharply defining their responsibilities, you will give your managers no choice but to focus on the business for which they are responsible and to tailor the business system to the particular success requirements in that business. They will have to focus on delivering the most value to customers at the least cost, and unless they develop competitive advantages they will fail. In other words, they will become more competitive because they must in order to succeed.

More Flexible

However, given the uncertainty of the environment, the pace of change, and the intensity of competition, you can not expect your institution to succeed in everything it tries. In an integrated bank holding company the failure of a part can bring down the whole enterprise. If the businesses can be self-contained, then so can the risks. Indeed, as the risks in the business become more transparent to the marketplace, the marketplace itself will begin to discipline those risks.

Your large bank is made up of hundreds of businesses, and as competition continues to intensify you can be sure to fail in many of them. But how do you get out of a business when the economics of the enterprise are all tied together? I have watched a number of banks try to shed businesses only to discover that they were shedding revenues but keeping most of the costs because those costs were shared among a wide variety of businesses.

By self-containing businesses, you can, in fact, place multiple bets on the future rather than one large integrated bet. This will enable you to sell off those businesses in which your people have failed to develop a sustaining competitive advantage and use the proceeds to invest behind those businesses in which your bank is winning.

More Valuable

Restructuring will not only make it possible for you to sell off parts of the institution; it will also increase their potential selling price. Rather than present a potential buyer with a conglomerate of activities, many of which it does not want, and with risks it does not understand, you can offer a discrete investment in a business with a particular set of unique revenues and a particular set of unique costs. This is the reason why relatively self-contained businesses, such as mortgage banking or credit card businesses, can command such extraordinary premiums when sold.

Whenever we do the analysis, we invariably discover that the parts of a large bank holding company are more valuable than the whole. In other words, if you were to restructure your institution into relatively self-contained, profitable businesses and then sell them all off, you would probably receive far more money than the current market capitalization of the company's stock. This condition occurs partly because today your bank's earnings are not transparent and because investors are reluctant to take "blind pool" risk , as I discussed earlier.

But it also occurs partly because many of the activities of most large banks actually destroy value. If you restructure your institution around its valuable activities, you can better identify those activities that are creating negative value. In fact, I believe you will probably add more value to shareholders over the next few years by simply working to eliminate activities that do not add value, once you know what they are.

A final point about value is that troubled institutions will increase their overall value by separating the problem part of their lending business from the rest of it and focusing some clear management attention on the solution of these asset problems. I will have more to say about this in the next chapter, in which I suggest more ways to move forward.

CHAPTER 13

CHARTING THE WAY: LARGER INSTITUTIONS

I believe almost every large bank has opportunities to play a number of very attractive roles in lending, deposit taking, and a wide variety of other areas as well. Many of these roles will involve specializing in not just a particular business but in particular subfunctions of particular businesses.

Before you can capture these opportunities, however, you must restructure your bank. It goes without saying that such restructuring is a deadly serious business. Once you have committed your institution, there will be no going back. You have a one-time opportunity to create the most value from your bank's historic franchise.

To me, this means that you must lead this restructuring with far greater care, and far greater discipline, than most bankers are used to. It is one thing to restructure an industrial company, which already has self-contained parts, such as discrete plants, discrete subsidiaries, and discrete property. It is quite another thing to transform a large financial institution, where all the costs are people and operating systems working together in an integrated, intertwined organization. To effect such massive organizational change, you need, not only a strategic vision, but also a detailed design of the reshaped organization, an effective means of communicating that design, detailed implementation plans, and a cadre of forceful leaders who are secure enough in their roles to drive home the change. And you will need time.

Let's begin with the strategic vision. What would you like to see your bank doing, say, five years from now? The best answer will, of course, respond to the unique circumstances of your individual institution. To develop that answer, you will certainly need to come to grips with how your bank will participate in the three fundamental roles of classic banking: (1) deposit taking and payments, (2) credit-risk taking, (3) and interest-risk taking. In addition, you must consider the many attractive specialized roles available in a wide variety of other activities. Once you have selected the roles, you will need to determine what role your overall holding company will play.

CLASSIC BANKING ROLES

I believe that many who lead large banks will find value in separating the broad deposit taking, credit-risk taking, and interest-rate risk taking functions, whether or not the government ever mandates "risk-free" depositories. These three major product functions are being driven by fundamentally different technological and competitive forces that are increasingly requiring specialized knowledge. For example, deposit taking is being driven not just by the paper-based processing technologies, but also by electronic and consumer outlet retailing (a la McDonalds) technologies. Lending is being driven increasingly by the securitized credit technologies, as described earlier, not to mention other new lending technologies (for example, some players are beginning to explore new artificial intelligence techniques, called *neural networks*, to separate out good credit applications from bad credit applications). Interest-risk taking is increasingly being driven by market-linkage technologies, such as interest-rate swaps, currency swaps, forwards, and futures.

Because the fundamental skills required for success in each of these three major functions are so different, you should seriously consider restructuring your bank holding company around them. That is, I believe you should consider having a general manager responsible for deposit taking, a general manager responsible for lending, and a general manager responsible for interest-rate risk taking across banks in a holding company. Bank holding companies with two large banks operating in two different states may find it more manageable to have two sets of these roles—that is, general managers for each functional role at each bank.

Because your business will be competing based on the value they add to customers, you should also look at restructuring options that focus on discrete customer needs. More and more, your bank will need to design tailored products and distribution systems for discrete segments (e.g., upscale, affluent, private banking, proprietors, small business, middle-corporate banking) in order to provide distinctive value. Thus, you may want specialized customer and product definitions that combine customer and discrete product cuts. For example, the lending businesses might be divided into customer/product specialized definitions such as home equity lending, credit card lending, middle-market lending, and so forth.

Finally, even within discrete customer/product groupings, some large banks may find value in specializing, and self-containing, even at the subfunctional level (e.g., credit card origination, credit card credit structuring, and credit card servicing).

In creating these roles, of course, you must always balance your desire for self-containment against economic realities. Shared costs will make sense at some level in each business. For example, a bank branch is an acceptable shared cost when it houses a number of deposit products and lending activities that could not individually justify the expense of the branch. Similarly, staff should be shared at some level to prevent duplication of support functions and unnecessary expense. Your design challenge will be to locate shared costs at a level where they create economies rather than inhibit or confuse business activity.

For example, can you enjoy the advantages of shared-cost economies at the branch level and still get functional specialization and autonomy? Let me suggest a variant of the approach I described in Chapter 11 for small banks. You could place the branch management function (and the geographic focus that goes with it) with the deposit-taking general manager, since the branch system is designed more for deposit taking than any other function; you could then dedicate specialized loan originators to the branch system. At that point, you would have two choices: First, you could keep the businesses at arms length by instructing the branch manager to act as a landlord to the loan originators, with the "rent" set according to what the lending function would have to pay elsewhere for similar accommodations. Alternatively, you could encourage a degree of collaboration by directing the origination function to share its origination income with the branch, on a fixed-percentage basis, for all the loan volume it generates. Some banks have already moved to a variant of this concept in which the only role of branches in lending is to accept loan applications.

As long as the federal government continues to subsidize risk taking in banks through federal deposit insurance, it will probably not be economic to fund many nonsecuritized loans in nonbank subsidiaries (that is, commercial finance companies)—even though some banks may decide to do it anyway to increase their flexibility. Should the government move to a "risk-free" depository concept, then it would be easy to convert the loan originators in the branches to holding company employees. At the end of the day, all of the loans originated by these employees could be booked in a specialized lending subsidiary of the holding company. This same subsidiary could also take first-loss risk on securitized credit transactions.

Of course, specialized lending units would originate loans through channels other than branches. For example, some of these specialized lending units might want to become "conduits" for smaller correspondent banks, as described in Chapter 11, or even for larger banks that lack skills in a particular form of securitized lending (e.g., trade receivable lending). Specialized lending groups would naturally develop other loan origination channels as well. For example, the leading credit card banks are already using such channels as direct mail and "affinity" groups to originate credit card applications.

Interest-rate risk taking would be managed by a centralized treasury function; many bank holding companies have already moved in this direction. The treasury would, of course, be responsible for balance sheet management, noncustomer assets (such as securities investments), and money market funding.

Of course, while you restructure, you will have to allow

for regulatory reality. Even though market forces are putting increasing pressure on the top managers of bank holding companies to carve out separate, functional roles in deposit taking, in various specialized lending asset categories, and in interest-rate risk taking, the regulatory structure currently works against this functional specialization. We are years away, even if the government endorsed the idea, from being able to convert today's banks to independent, functionally specialized subsidiaries as was described in Chapter 8. Thus, deposit taking, credit-risk taking, and interest-risk taking must inevitably share the same bank balance sheet for some time to come, even if they have discrete revenues and expense bases.

How do you then measure the economic performance of the three different functions so they can operate with autonomy? In other words, how do you divide up the net interest margin, and who bears what capital costs when the functions will continue to share the same balance sheet?

We have found some approaches that help. For example, we have found it helpful to use a risk-free, matched-funded opportunity rate (MOR) to transfer interest income and interest expense between units (as also discussed in Chapter 10). Under this approach lending units are charged for funds at an appropriate risk-free funding rate. For example, a revolving credit that reprices every six months is charged for funds at the bank's six-month certificate of deposit rate. Similarly, deposits are credited at an appropriate risk-free return consistent with their maturity. For example, core retail demand deposits might be credited with the five-year treasury note rate to reflect their stability. The difference between these artificial transfer rates and the bank's actual funding costs and lending spreads—that is, the profits and losses earned from mismatching and funding—are credited to treasury.

Capital allocation is even easier: All you need to do is apply the new Federal Reserve capital equity guidelines since, like it or not, they define how much capital you need. Once equity capital is allocated to a business, using these guidelines, you charge each unit for equity used based upon an estimate of the bank holding company's cost of equity capital. For example, if the equity costs of the bank were 16 percent after tax, and a unit used $100 million of equity capital, it would be charged $16 million for the use of that capital. Under this approach deposit-taking units wind up with relatively low capital allocations, while treasury and lending units wind up with relatively large allocations. Allocating the appropriate costs of equity capital to lending units is particularly important. Unless these units feel the pain of unrealistically high capital guidelines, they will have insufficient incentive to securitize their loans to save the capital costs.

As the flow of funds becomes more and more securitized, economics will become more and more self-contained—with or without regulatory change.

OTHER SELF-CONTAINED ROLES

There are a variety of other major, self-contained product functional roles (in addition to deposit taking, lending, and interest-risk taking) that the top managers of some large banking institutions may want to consider. These include: (1) investment management, (2) merchant banking and corporate finance, (3) servicing loans and other service bureau functions, and (4) distributing, trading, and brokering securities. As you evaluate these roles, however, you should keep in mind that they are already covered, most of them very well, by nonbanks and that few banks today have all the skills they would need to perform them.

Investment Management

The more the flow of funds is securitized, the greater will be the need, by definition, for investment management. Money that would have flowed into banks as deposits will need to find other channels, such as money market and bond mutual funds. Therefore, the mutual funds investment management opportunities should be substantial. Regulation permitting, and there already is considerable freedom in this area, I would expect many banks to use their branches to raise money to be placed into these funds. I would also expect many banks to distribute mutual funds through a wide variety of nonbranch channels such as the mail. If you enter this business, though, you should be prepared to have plenty of competition from existing securities firms (like Merrill Lynch and Shearson Lehman) and mutual fund companies (like Fidelity and Dreyfus).

Merchant Banking and Corporate Finance

As loan margins narrow and as corporate loans are increasingly securitized, many corporate banks will need to rethink their role in servicing corporations. Most seem to be gravitating towards a role that combines merchant banking and corporate finance and that includes such services as mergers and acquisitions, "mezzanine" (or quasi-equity) finance, and (regulation permitting) equity finance. Frankly, the nation will not need as many of these merchant banks as there are institutions with ambition to create them. But I suspect this will not deter many who find it difficult to envision their institution without this business. Many merchant banks will therefore be uneconomic. On the other hand, if you self-contain your merchant banking activities as a holding company subsidiary, you will probably create value even if your merchant bank "fails" because you will be able to sell the business to another "winning" merchant bank.

Servicing Loans and Other Service Bureau Functions

The disaggregation of the lending business system will create a need in each category of lending for service bureaus to collect loans, process payments, and keep track of who owns what cash flow in securitized credit transactions. You might find such a role very attractive, if your bank is positioned to be a very large player; it probably will take several billion dollars' worth of servicing value in a particular category of loan to be scale effective. Consequently, I would expect that relatively few players will wind up dominating the servicing business for each loan category.

In addition to loan servicing, there will also be service bureau functional roles for nearly every service now provided by a bank—including, for example, payments processing, foreign exchange processing, custody and safekeeping, and trade services.

As companies such as ADP have proven, service bureau businesses can be very attractive in areas like payroll processing. But they require far greater skill in operations and systems than most internal bank operations and systems staffs have. Because most of these internally oriented units have grown up with a captive source of volume, from their own bank, they often lack both the cost-effectiveness and the customer service orientation required to win in the service bureau business.

Distributing, Trading, and Brokering Securities

Many bankers are looking forward to the breakdown of Glass-Steagall barriers because they perceive opportunities in distributing, trading, and brokering securities. For some there undoubtedly will be significant opportunities. But any top manager considering these roles should realize that the securities industry has also been developing considerable overcapacity, and simply adding more capacity is unlikely to be a winning strategy for anyone. If you want your bank to win, you must find a way to use your new powers, if you get them, to do something different for customers than is currently being done by securities firms. If your bank simply emulates someone like Merrill Lynch, you will add little value to customers and will almost certainly fail.

I am concerned, too, that some bankers simply do not realize how different the securities business is from the banking business and how different, and complex, the risks are. As a result, I believe that many of them will find it more difficult to enter these securities functions than they expect. For many it will prove to be an unwise venture.

HOLDING COMPANY ROLES

Once you have created self-contained business around viable roles, you will of course still need to manage the resulting collection of businesses, that is, the corporation as a whole

(Exhibit 13-1). Many people wrongly assume that if you self-contain individual business, you give up synergies. This need not happen, if you adopt a model of corporate management that is already widely used outside of banking: a holding company, managed by people who are independent of the management of individual businesses.

The holding company I propose is quite different from today's typical bank holding company, which is difficult to distinguish from a bank. In the wake of the Bank Holding Company Act of 1970, most banks simply formed a holding company as a legal shell to own themselves. The holding company raised capital; it also enabled the bank to engage, through essentially shell subsidiaries, in a variety of activities that were either inconvenient to perform in the bank or prohibited by regulation from being performed by the bank. Thus, for most players the holding company became an extension of the bank. Generally, the top management of the bank was also the top management of the holding company. And usually, the same staff support served both the bank and the holding company.

In multibank, or chain, holding companies like First Interstate, Norwest, and Bay Banks, the situation is somewhat different, in that these contain a number of self-contained banks. But again, it is difficult to distinguish holding company activity from bank activity, since the management of the biggest bank in the chain tends to be relatively indistinguishable from that of the holding company.

In place of this model, I propose a structure more like such nonbank holding companies as American Express (which owns American Express, Shearson Lehman, IDS, the American Express Bank, etc.), General Electric (which owns GECC, Kidder, Peabody, etc.) and Sears (which owns Allstate, Dean Witter, etc.). In addition, at least one major bank holding company, Security Pacific, operates close to the model I'm proposing.

Under this model, the role of the holding company is to focus on corporate, as opposed to business, management. The role of business management is to build and maintain a competitive advantage over others engaged in the same business, that is, to win in that business. In contrast, the role of holding company corporate management is to maximize shareholder wealth.

EXHIBIT 13–1
Holding Company Model of Corporate Management

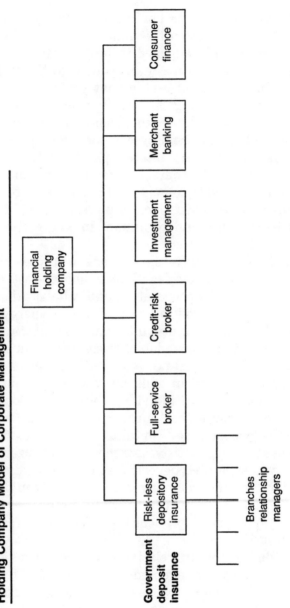

To perform this role the holding company management must be a little detached from the underlying operating businesses. If your mind is fully engaged in how to beat competitors in a business, it is hard to maintain your objectivity. Emotion can often get in the way of seeing that you are fighting a losing battle. I am not arguing that holding company corporate management should not know the business; rather, I mean that it is essential for the holding company corporate management to keep the shareholders' interest paramount. Conveniently for those who do it well, shareholders' interests and top management interests tend to coincide. The turnover rate of bank holding company chief executives is increasing rapidly, and stock price is increasingly a determinant in who will acquire others and who will be acquired.

A holding company like the one I propose can be a better guarantor of synergies than a shared-cost organization, because it can make cooperation and collaboration formal and systematic. In a shared-cost organization synergy depends too much on physical proximity, informal processes, and good will— which are often not dependable. In contrast, a financial holding company can use formal powers to add enormous value to self-contained businesses. In addition to raising capital and funding more cheaply than individual businesses could, a holding company can ensure that appropriate alliances are forged between the various self-contained businesses that possess complementary competitive strengths. For example, assuming that you separated deposit taking from lending as described earlier, holding company management could ensure that loan originators from the lending product function were placed in appropriate branches and that the "rent" they paid was appropriate.

The distinction in relative roles between operating and holding company management seems obvious to nonbankers. But I find that many top bank managers do not understand the distinction, since most combine corporate and operating roles. Many top bank managers push responsibility for operating results down to line managers but keep for themselves control of many of the staff functions required to operate. Moreover, they are often so emotionally committed to certain businesses that they feel no compunction about allowing, or indeed encouraging, massive cross-subsidization—often through biasing the funds transfer rate, cost allocations, and capital allocations.

If you are too emotionally close to the business, it is difficult to ask the tough questions. Are we achieving profits simply by taking too much risk? Are we milking businesses we should be investing in? Are we really developing the capabilities we need for long-term success, or are we sacrificing the future for another quarter's earnings? Do we have a realistic chance of winning? Are we subsidizing businesses we should either fix or sell? It is also difficult to be an honest broker between the businesses, ensuring that relationships between businesses are fair to all parties.

Presently, many who manage bank holding companies get corporate and business management roles confused, because individual businesses are not sufficiently self-contained. As I suggested in Chapter 12, bankers have trouble doing either job right because they are simultaneously trying to make operating decisions based on insufficient information and knowledge *as well as* focus on corporate strategy, corporate management, and corporate policy issues. At the same time, the lack of self-containment causes operating managers to have too little freedom to operate and to have too limited a scope to build the general management capabilities they need. Consequently, top managers and operating managers become frustrated with each other.

TAKING ACTION

As the top manager of a large bank or bank holding company, you face a tremendous task. The course you set and the speed and skill with which you guide your institution toward its goal will determine whether your institution is still a force to be reckoned with, say, 10 years from now.

Some are tempted to do nothing about restructuring because they plan to be sitting on a sailboat 10 years from now, having paid their dues. Others are beginning to see so much pressure on their economics that they are beginning to think they had better do something different, soon. For them the question is: Where do I start?

If you are holding off, I have a word of caution. Your institution is not as agile as the small banks are. Most small banks could restructure their relatively simple activities in a year or less; because your institution is so much more complex, the same task will take you from three to five years—assuming you have the financial strength to give yourself that much time to do it carefully and right. Your nonbank, value-based competitors are not waiting around. Your window of opportunity will shut sooner or later. Thus, I would advise you to start moving now, regulatory uncertainty and all, if you want your institution to be in the game longer term.

If you are under pressure now, or if you will feel that pressure in the months ahead, I have another concern. It is human nature to look for a quick fix. But in this situation acting too quickly will be as dangerous as acting too late. Your first idea may not be right, and it could be destructive if it involves getting rid of activities that are potentially a source of strength. You may not have the three to five years to play with that some of your brethren in strong regionals have. But you have got to be as deliberate and thorough as you possibly can be, because at this point false moves are forever.

How then should you move ahead? The general steps will be the same whether your institution is in trouble or relatively strong. The main difference will be in the depth and level of detail at which you work.

Your first step should be to develop the will to act, as described in Chapter 10. You should then lead your people through a rigorous examination of your institution and its position in the marketplace. You must understand its real economics, as described in Chapter 10. Look at the pieces of your organization: What skills are located in each group? What tasks are being performed now?

You next turn to an assessment of your institution's fundamental competitive strengths and weaknesses, business by business. Make sure you get the perspectives of objective, friendly outsiders. Speak to customers, directors, your institution's lawyers and accountants. Ask them: What are we good at? What are our competitors doing? Where are we winning? Where are we losing? As you conduct these valuable interviews, remember that it is no use asking questions unless you are ready to really listen and then vigorously synthesize the answers.

Having completed your internal and external assessment, your next challenge will be to determine viable, long-term roles your bank could perform—that is, where your bank has a realistic opportunity to develop and sustain a competitive advantage. For each role you should be able to define major product functions, geography, customers, and business system. I suspect a super regional might have roughly a dozen candidates for ongoing, self-contained, potentially viable roles; a healthy money center bank might have 20 to 30; a struggling institution would obviously have fewer options, because it lacks the strength to invest behind many new roles. The end product of this effort would be a strategic vision for the corporation that is something more than the sum of its various roles and that is likely to be different in each individual case.

Once you have defined your vision in terms of ongoing, viable business roles, you will be ready to begin the real task: the detailed design and planning work that will make your vision a reality through a simultaneous stripping away and building up of capabilities. Most large bank holding companies that do not have massive credit problems today probably contain the makings of a highly profitable, highly viable institution. They have most of the skills and other capabilities they need to succeed. But they are also carrying a great many activities that are destroying value. Your job now will be to develop a plan for removing everything that is not needed to realize your vision, without destroying the skills and customer franchise your new vision requires for success. It is a bit like when Michelangelo addressed a block of fine marble; his task was to remove everything that did not look like David. The tool he needed was a chisel, not a sledgehammer. Moreover, he needed time and a great deal of skill. If you are not willing and able to take the time and do it right, you should probably consider selling your block of marble to someone else. The alternative, an attempt to restructure in a hurry, could leave you standing in the middle of a pile of dust.

At this point the paths of the healthy and the struggling large bank holding companies diverge somewhat. If you are leading a healthy institution, you can concentrate on designing businesses around the roles that comprise your vision of the future. If I were you, I would begin the design effort by selecting three or four of your major potential self-contained businesses and putting my best candidates for running each one, along with teams of three to five people each, in charge of an effort to design a way of winning in that business. I would then hand them a clean piece of paper and challenge them to design a business system that enables the business to deliver substantially more value to its target set of customers than existing and potential competitors, at significantly less cost (that is, 30 to 40 percent less). We at McKinsey have found that such challenges cause people to push their thinking; you can not meet such a challenge by thinking on a business-as-usual basis. Then once a concept has been designed, you should challenge it. The burden of proof should rest with the design team, and if the design is not good enough, you should send the team back to the drawing board. In many cases this process will force them to revisit the definition of the business itself. In other cases the team may decide it is really unrealistic to compete in the business at all. And in some cases you may end up rethinking your vision for the entire corporation.

If you are leading a struggling institution, you must simultaneously address your current credit problems and your need to restructure. You will obviously need to devote a good deal of your own attention—as well as some of your most capable people—to simply stopping weak lending practices and managing the problematic part of your loan portfolio. One of the most important parts of this process is to separate the bad parts of the loan portfolio from the strong parts, perhaps through use of the "liquidity bank" approach described earlier. All this work on the problem loans will, of course, limit the resources you can apply right now to realizing a fundamentally different vision for the future of your institution. On the other hand, your success at managing through your credit problems will determine how long you have to work on restructuring, or do business of any kind. Thus, it will make sense for you to concentrate on more modest restructuring goals for now—including fewer roles— while you work out current business problems. In some cases your work may honestly be aimed at maximizing the selling price of your institution, rather than strengthening its future competitive position. Here most of the major restructuring work will be carried out in the context of another institution.

Let's return to the program of the top manager whose institution is strong enough to contemplate an independent, vital vision of the future. Once one of your teams has developed a viable concept for a potential self-contained business, you should direct the team to go to the blueprint level of detail by defining a business strategy and a "managing concept," including roles, processes, and organization structure.

Based on the blueprint, the team should prepare a detailed implementation plan to get from where the organization is to where it needs to be. In my experience, it takes from 4 to 6 months to go from a business concept to a completed, detailed implementation plan; it can easily take 18 months to 24 months to implement a full business restructuring plan completely.

I would replicate this process for every major business, taking no more than three or four at a time, until I was done. It is a lot of work, but it is necessary. It should be approached with all the seriousness of building a new building. Attention to detail is essential.

Of course, it is difficult to both tear down and build from the ground up at the same time. Preserving existing economics while building a core business is difficult under the best of circumstances. That is the reason why I believe your design effort should be off-line. In selecting businesses to self-contain I would try to start with those businesses that have the *least* to do with the traditional deposit and lending core functions, since the core functions will be hardest to address and will contain the greatest threat to the core earnings stream. Indeed, the way to get to a risk-free depository system is to simply remove, piece by piece, everything that does not look like a risk-free depository. If you wait until the last step to unbundle your deposit function from your lending functions, you will give the securitized credit technology time to mature and, hopefully, the regulatory environment time to become more certain.

As you create your various self-contained businesses, you will begin to expose a lot of unnecessary costs. Shedding these costs, either by selling units or closing them down, can help buy your institution valuable time.

In summary, it is essential to remember that the keys to

success are: (1) to have a group of managers who are secure enough in their roles to drive home the change, (2) to develop and sustain a clear vision of where the institution is headed, and (3) to be rigorous in your approach, with particular attention to detailed implementation planning.

Given the magnitude of the undertaking, I do not expect all bankers to approach restructuring as carefully and thoroughly as I propose. I suspect that some will never develop the will to act at all and that others will succumb to the temptation to act too quickly. The lucky ones, however, are indeed equipped to approach restructuring with the care and the energy I have just described. You have real opportunities to emerge with a leading institution in a transformed financial system. I believe, at the end of the day, the smart people who work hard will win.

TECHNICAL AND METHODOLOGICAL NOTE AND REFERENCE

Discussion of bank regulation has become a particularly fertile field, and there are a number of important contributors to the debate. Many of these contributors are developing a consensus around some of the ideas discussed in the book (e.g., functional regulation, moving to a "risk-free," or "safe," bank concept prompt reorganization of troubled institutions and allowing financial holding companies to own both depository and nondepository subsidiaries). The actual proposals made by different individuals are very different in their details. No attempt has been made in the book to debate or elaborate on these proposals by others. To do so would require a book by itself.

The model closest to the model proposed in this book is the financial holding company and "safe" bank model proposed by Robert E. Litan of the Brookings Institute in his excellent book *What Should Banks Do?* Other important proposals include a new model for a "functional" system of regulation and protection of the payment system that was introduced in 1987 by Gerald Corrigan, President of the Federal Reserve Bank of New York in *Financial Markets Structure: A Longer View*. Another model has been proposed by George Bentson and George Kaufman, in a book to be published shortly, called *Restructuring Banking and Financial Services in America;* they advocate, among other things, a model based on requiring institutions to maintain adequate capital using a "market value" of assets approach and timely reorganization of troubled institutions. Chairman William Seidman of the FDIC has made *de facto* proposals about the role of the holding companies through his handling of failing banks and has proposed his own model for financial institution regulation. He and his staff have also pushed the thinking on the "bridge bank" structure. A "bridge bank" is an interim bank used to facilitate the restructuring of a bank that would otherwise be liquidated. Bert Ely has written extensively on the thrift crisis and the problems of federal deposit insurance. On the lighter side, anyone who wants to understand the dangers of unsound lending practices should read Mark Singer's *Funny Money*, which provides a detailed account of the Penn Square/Continental Illinois debacle. In addition to these sources, students of the debate have literally hundreds of articles and books from which to choose. A few of these, particularly those discussing a "fail-safe" bank, are listed at the end of this note.

Much of the information in this book is derived from interview and client experience. However, a surprising degree of information came from a thorough reading of the financial press, which has become progressively more professional, more complete, and more insightful over the last few years. In addition to the coverage of the issues by the *Wall Street Journal*, the *New York Times, Business Week, Fortune, The Economist, Institutional Investor, Euromoney,* and the *Financial Times,* I've found it to be particularly helpful to read the *Asset Sales Report,* which provides new weekly developments in securitized credit. One of the advantages of being part of a large consulting firm is that many of my colleagues have kept their eyes open for relevant information and articles and have been of enormous help in keeping me abreast of events. This help was particularly important in keeping abreast of articles appearing in the industry's daily "bible" *The American Banker.*

Close readers of the book will observe that no attempt has been made to deal with either the corporate finance or monetary policy implications of the recommendations in this book. I decided that these issues were beyond the scope of the book.

A brief methodological note is needed on the sources of information on commercial banks. Most of the commercial bank data used in this book were taken directly from reports of the FDIC. The numbers are for U.S. commercial banking entities and do not include earnings or assets of nonbank subsidiaries of bank holding companies.

For analysis purposes (e.g., determining the amount of assets held by regional banks), we combined groups owned by a single holding company into a single entity. Banks not belonging to any bank holding company were treated as separate, standalone organizations. Hence, we arrived at a universe of roughly 10,700 banking organizations—6,000 holding companies (composed of over 9,000 individual banks) and 4,700 banks that are not owned by a holding company.

The banks were then categorized according to asset size. "Local" banks include organizations with assets of less than $100 million; "community" banks include organizations with $100 million to $1 billion in assets; and "regional" refers to all nonmoney center banks with assets over $1 billion. Money center banks, for all years, are designated to include the following: Bankers Trust, Chase Manhattan, Chemical New York, Citicorp, Continental Illinois, First Chicago, Irving Bank, J.P. Morgan, Manufacturers Hanover, and Security Pacific.

No attempt has been made to restate data from prior years to reflect mergers and acquisitions: If a local bank was acquired by a regional bank holding company, it simply "disappears" from the local bank categorization at that point. Similarly, if a local bank's assets grew from, say, $99 million to $101 million over the course of a year, it was treated as a community bank during the year.

For two pragmatic reasons, most of our analysis was done on results through 1986 rather than 1987. First, the year-end numbers for 1987 were not available in time. Second, 1987 numbers were distorted by the large provisioning for LDC debt.

Readers who were disappointed that the data analysis of the savings and loan industry was not as rigorous as that of commercial banks must realize that the problem is that the underlying FSLIC data are less complete, less accessible, and less accurate that FDIC data. We saw no point in over-analyzing poor-quality data.

BIBLIOGRAPHY

Angermueller, James J. "Statement" before a Subcommittee of the Committee on Government Operations, Structure and Regulation of Financial Firms and Holding Companies (Part 3). *Hearings,* U.S. Congress. House. 99th Cong., 2nd sess., 1987, pp. 4–16.

Bentson, George J., and George G. Kaufman. *Risk and Solvency Regulation of Depository Institutions.* Federal Reserve Bank of Chicago, SM 88–1.

Bryan, Lowell L. "The Credit Bomb in our Financial System," *The Harvard Business Review,* January, 1987, pp. 45–51.

Bryan, Lowell L. "Securitized Credit. The Potential for a Sounder, more Effective Financial System," Hearings before the Committee on Banking, Housing, and Urban Affairs. United States Senate, One Hundredth Congress. October 13 and 14, 1987 (S. HRG. 100–481).

Copeland, Thomas E., and J. Fred Weston. *Financial Theory and Corporate Policy.* Reading, MA: Addison-Wesley, 1979. (Discusses some of the cost of equity issues.)

Corrigan, E. Gerald. *Financial Market Structure: A Longer View.* Federal Reserve Bank of New York, 1987.

Friedman, Milton and Anna J. Schwartz. *A Monetary History of the United States, 1867–1960.* Princeton: Princeton University Press, 1963.

Kareken, John H. "Federal Bank Regulatory Policy." *Journal of Business,* January 1984, pp. 3–48.

Lawrence, Robert J. "Minimizing Regulation of the Financial Services Industry." *Issues in Bank Regulation,* Summer 1985, pp. 22–30.

Litan, Robert E. *What Should Banks Do?* Washington, DC: Brookings Institute, 1987.

Modigliai, F., and M. H. Miller. "The Cost of Capital, Corporation Finance, and the Theory of Investment." *American Economic Review*, June 1958, pp. 261–297. (This is the seminal piece on the cost of capital.)

Rosenthal, James and Juan Ocampo, *Securitization of Credit: Inside the New Technology of Finance.* New York: John Wiley & Sons, Inc., (in press).

Singer, Mark. *Funny Money.* New York: Knopf, 1985.

Tobin, James. "Financial Innovation and Deregulation Perspective." In *Financial and Monetary Policy: Asia and the West*, ed. Y. Suzuki and H. Yomo. Tokyo: University of Tokyo Press, 1986, pp. 31–42.

INDEX